What Peo
Abou

Brings Lean back to the level of simplicity that should have never gone away from the original concepts.

Sammy Obara, Principle, Honsha Associates

Proves that Lean is more than just a business process, it is truly a way of life that can help us in everything we do.

Craig Germain, President, XTL Logistics Inc.

Explores the essence of Lean philosophy, reminding us that with curiosity, creativity, and discipline, we can all achieve our own variety of excellence.

Thomas Goldsby, Ph.D., Lean educator and author

An excellent source to help your organization begin thinking about and understanding just what it means to implement and become Lean. Creates the critical thinking to get your Lean transformation off to the right start!

Jim Huntzinger, President, Lean Accounting Summit

An entertaining way to help your organization appreciate the broad possibilities to apply Lean and the tremendously positive impact it can have with suppliers, customers, and within the company.

Mark Richards, President, AWI (Associated Warehouses Inc.)

From the front office to the shop floor, this is the book everybody in your organization should read!

John Rickerby, President, First Concrete Ltd.

Illustrates how fundamental the application of Lean is for people to learn, develop, and grow.

Steven T. Gran, Principal, Blueprint 57

Weaves Lean principles into an experience everyone can relate to. No matter how far along you are on your Lean Journey, this book has something for you. This should be required reading for all organizations.

Steve Scholten, Logistics Professional

Shows how Lean is simply an extension of common sense. A pleasant mix of narrative and Lean theory. Great read!

Matt Klaric, President, St. Louis CSCMP Roundtable

Everything I Know About Lean

I Learned in First Grade

Robert O. Martichenko

Illustrations by Liz Maute

Foreword by Pascal Dennis

Proudly printed in the United States of America.
Signature Book Printing, www.sbpbooks.com

ISBN: 978-0-615-21969-1

To obtain copies of this book, contact:

LeaninFirstGrade@Leancor.com

www.leancor.com

Dedications

To my daughters Emilee June and Abigail Lillian Jane

In memory of my grandmother, Mary Wright, an inspirational teacher in and out of school.

With heartfelt gratitude to June Martichenko and Jane Young, who chose teaching our children as their life work. You both make a significant impact in the lives of countless children.

Liz Maute's illustrations are dedicated to her grandmother, Marjorie P. Maute, who passed away during this book project. She had a wise demeanor and was always up to something. Grammy Maute had a fabulous costume jewelry collection, which included a large vintage owl necklace. Liz wore the necklace at all times while creating this original and beautiful set of pictures to support our story.

Acknowledgments

Completing this book was not possible without the help of many people. You know who you are and I sincerely appreciate your time, expertise, and friendship.

To my friends who reviewed the text and offered incredibly valuable comments. Thank you to Sue Armstrong, Tim Conrad, Craig Germain, Thomas and Kathie Goldsby, Steven Gran, David Greathouse, Ben Green, Richard Holland, Jim Huntzinger, Matt Klaric, Ronald Kulker, Tamara Nelson, Sammy Obara, Mark Richards, John Rickerby, Pamela Ruebusch, Stephen Scholten, Gary Vance, Mark Wallace, Mark Wheeler, Helen Zak, and Ramin Zarrabi.

Thanks to the LeanCor team and, in particular, the support of Jack Hines and Glen Wright.

A sincere thank you to all LeanCor customers. You allow us to prove that by focusing on the basics we can achieve significant results.

I also acknowledge the years of conversation with Jim Luckman, Guy Parsons, and Pascal Dennis. Your insights and questions about *my* questions led to the creation of this story.

Thanks to my friend Elijah Ray for continuously reminding me about true priorities.

Specifically with the writing and printing of the book, I want to thank Corinne Hines, Dr. June Martichenko, Andrew Teteris, Phil Nanzetta, Sarah Nelson, Liz Maute, Denis Drever, and Sue Reynard. The cover should, in fact, have Sue's and June's name on it.

Thanks to Sam and Gary Francis for allowing me to print the words to the Henry Ford song. Their mission at www.classroomclassics.com is to teach children basic moral values and patriotism through music.

And last, but certainly not least, my sincere appreciation to Miss Lindsey Spjut, Abbey's first grade teacher. Your open door hospitality during my "go see" stage of writing made all the difference. You are an amazing teacher.

Contents

Foreword

When my friend and colleague Robert Martichenko told me he'd written a primer on Lean, I was pleased and supportive. Robert is a man of boundless energy and enthusiasm, and I knew he'd come up with something interesting.

Robert has produced an engaging and accessible overview of what W. Edwards Deming called the "profound system of knowledge." Join Robert, Emilee, Abbey, and Orlo the Wise Old Owl as they discover the basics of Lean in a first grade class.

As it happens, my wife teaches grade school and I can confirm that we do indeed learn 5 S, visual management, and the other Lean basics at a young age.

Why do we forget? Good question…

Enjoy the book.

Pascal Dennis

19 June 2008

Introduction

As president of LeanCor LLC and a committed Lean practitioner, I have the pleasure of working with many organizations on their Lean Journeys. When businesses begin their journeys, the most important step is to educate the entire organization on the fundamentals of Lean thinking. That is the purpose of this book. This book is a simple and fun approach to the key concepts and tools that support the Lean Enterprise.

For some time, I searched for an analogy that would best illustrate Lean concepts. The analogy that forms this narrative was revealed to me during a visit to my youngest daughter's first grade classroom. It was all there.

We do not need to overcomplicate Lean principles. Successful Lean Journeys are achieved by organizations that understand that the complexity of Lean is in its simplicity: to have a plan, do the plan, check the plan, and then adjust to improve upon the plan. Yet we continue to ask: why are Lean principles so difficult for organizations to understand and to execute effectively?

From my experience, I have concluded that the single most important aspect of sustained Lean success and operational excellence is to understand this is a way of thinking. Some of you may read this book and believe it describes a set of tools to be used to eliminate waste in work processes. While the narrative does introduce what are known as Lean tools, the tools themselves are not the end game. What is useful about a tool if you don't understand the principle and value it brings?

Lean tools were developed to solve specific organizational problems. Each Lean tool supports a solution for a particular business problem. Yet companies attempt to implement Lean tools without clearly understanding what problems they are trying to solve! Which begs the question of why we would want to solve problems in the first place. The reason is to make the organization stronger. Make no mistake, Lean is about serving our customers better, increasing revenues, and reducing costs. While the term "Lean Journey" has now taken on almost philosophical connotations, let us not forget this is about improving the business. This is about results.

Organizations struggle with their Lean Journeys because they focus only on Lean tools and do not spend enough time thinking about and understanding Lean principles. For example, is one-piece flow a tool for inventory reduction or is it a fundamental way of thinking that shows us the way to ignore economies of scale and begin focusing on problem identification and waste elimination?

Lean is not about tools, it is about thinking. Every single member of the organization needs to come to work and think about a better way to get things done. We need to think about our work, we need to experiment with new ideas, and we need to learn from these experiments. This is the Lean way. Tools are about *how*, but thinking is about *why*! Without knowing why you would implement Lean, the how will never be sustained.

The following story has two components. First, there is the fact-inspired but fictional narrative of my time with Abbey in her first grade class. This is about spending time doing the right things and having your eyes open to see what is going on in your environment.

Second, each chapter ends with a summary from Orlo the Wise Old Owl. I have a personal attachment to Orlo, as he is named after my grandfather (actually spelled Orloe, which is also my middle name). Orlo also represents the side of us that knows what we need to do to improve. With all certainty, the seeds to fix organizational problems already rest inside the organization. We simply need to allow employees to cultivate those seeds. When we create the environment of continuous improvement and continuous learning, that is what we call a Lean Enterprise. Orlo helps us to understand how we can accomplish the task of creating a Lean Enterprise.

To the reader, I thank you for your time. My hope is that time spent with these story characters is value-added to your day. But beware! You too may fall into the same trap I did. Once the Lean bug has bitten, you are unable to function in society without looking for process waste and ideas for improvement. This can be a curse.

Personally, I do try to turn it off, but when that is impossible, I listen to Orlo the Owl, a voice in my head. I suppose if one is forced to hear a little (and at times annoying) voice, it could be worse than listening to Orlo the Wise Old Owl.

Enjoy the book, and, as my friend Sue Reynard would say, do what your spirit calls you to do.

First Day of First Grade

7:30 A.M.

Every day is a good day, but some are better than others. I sense this will be one of those days—a day like no other.

"Wake up, honey. It's time to get up for your first day of school," I say to my daughter Abbey. As long as I live, I'll never forget the look on Abbey's face as she rubs her eyes and smiles up at me knowing that today is the big day—her first day of first grade. Not only that, but her dad has been granted permission to go with her to school for the whole day.

Over breakfast, Abbey's big sister, Emilee, and her mom, Corinne, coach her on the ins and outs of going to school full time. Neither Abbey nor I really listen; we smile at each other knowing that together we can get through anything. Heck, how hard can it be to go to first grade? Sometimes not knowing all the rules can be an adventure. Sometimes you just have to go with the flow and see what the day brings.

For me personally, today is a day to stop thinking about work and to spend some time with my daughter. As I watch my two daughters at the breakfast table, I can't help but think about the last ten years. Over a decade ago, my wife and I made the momentous decision to move from Canada to the United States. I was given the opportunity to participate in a start-up of a green field Toyota Motor Manufacturing facility. As a supply chain professional, this opportunity was too good to be true. The Toyota experience is where my Lean Journey began and it influenced my professional and personal lives in many ways. Since then, I have not looked back as my interest in Lean continues to grow. In fact, I've been accused of taking Lean principles a little too seriously and a little too far into my household. "Don't you ever stop thinking about Lean?" are words that I hear many times from family members. Today is not about Lean, today is a day to clear my mind of work and to spend time with Abbey.

Even though I am driving to Abbey's school, her mother and I want her to experience the school bus ride with her sister. I promise to follow the bus and to meet them both at the front door of the school. Kneeling down in front of little Abbey, Corinne pins a cardboard bumblebee on her shirt that says "First Day of First Grade."

"Ah!" I say to Corinne, "I like the sign. Are those new? I don't remember Emilee having one when she started first grade."

"The school started using them last year," answers Corinne. "They make it easier for everyone in the school—students, teachers, and support staff—to tell which kids are first graders and may need extra help." She pulls something else from a bag and hands it to me. "This is for you to wear."

It is a strap to go around my neck with a card that says "Parent Visitor" on it. "What's this?" I ask.

"You need to wear that at the school," Corinne answers. "Same idea as Abbey's bumblebee—this is used to identify visiting parents."

I am about to comment on the excellent use of visual management when I hear my daughters in the front hall. "C'mon, Dad, we'll be late!" yells Abbey, who is already halfway out the door.

Her mother and I follow Abbey out the door, and I turn to Corinne to ask what time the bus is scheduled to arrive, hoping I don't sound like the out-of-touch father I sometimes resemble.

"Eight twenty-two," she responds. "It's posted in the local newspaper, remember? I showed it to you last night." She punctuates her remark with an elbow to my ribs.

"Can they really be that precise?" I ask.

"I think they've studied how much time it takes based on the number of kids on the route," says Corinne. "That is tight timing, but I guess they have to plan it that way considering all the stops and kids they have to pick up."

We reach the bus stop along with other parents and neighborhood kids. There are several groups of students, some going to the high school, others going to the middle school, and then there are the children heading to Williams Elementary. Thinking out loud I say, "I hope Abbey and Emilee get on the right bus."

A yellow school bus arrives and Abbey, excited as she is, heads for the bus door. The driver quickly notes her bumblebee identification card and says, "Your bus is on its way, young lady. This bus is headed to Daniel County High School." Abbey runs back to me, students file onto the bus, and it moves on. Soon the right bus appears and the students for Williams Elementary School get on. It is reassuring to see that the identification plan prevented Abbey from getting on the wrong bus. While cameras click, our precious cargo boards the bus, and so begins Abbey's first full day of school.

Orlo the Wise Old Owl

... on Visual Management

If a visitor were to walk into your workplace—be it an office or a factory floor—could they identify the steps in your work process just by looking around? If your boss came by, could he or she tell the status of the things you're working on just by looking?

The ability to tell *at a glance* what the work is and the status of each work step is called "visual management." Making work visible is the first step toward being able to understand and improve it.

That's why a Lean Enterprise focuses on making the workplace a visual environment. You need to design systems and processes filled with visual cues to let you know what the plan is, how much work is "in process" at any given moment, and what the status of that work is.

Visuals allow you to see and instantly know when you have a problem or abnormal condition. Visual

management will help you to *error-proof* your processes by visually showing when something is not right. This is known by the Japanese term **Poka Yoke** (pronounced POH-ka YO-keh). Ideally, Poka Yoke is a simple and inexpensive system or visual cue that will highlight errors before or as they happen. For example, in Abbey's case, a simple card provided the bus driver with a visual cue that she was about to get on the wrong bus. Because of the Poka Yoke, that error was prevented and Abbey got on the right bus.

Creating a situation where errors are prevented (or immediately caught before being passed on) is known in the Lean environment as **quality at the source**. This is in sharp contrast to old-fashioned "quality control" or "quality assurance" measures that focus on catching errors *after* they are produced and passed on to the next step in the process.

Quality at the source teaches us that there is a big difference between a mistake and a defect. Mistakes are just mistakes. A defect is when a mistake is handed on to the next process or to the end customer. We know that if human beings are involved, mistakes will certainly happen. However, if we use visual cues to help error-proof our processes, we can detect *potential* mistakes before they occur and prevent *actual* mistakes from being passed on to the customer.

Three Lessons on Visual Management

- Make your work and the status of that work as visual as possible
- Design simple and inexpensive techniques to error-proof processes
- Catch mistakes and errors before they turn into customer defects

8:30 A.M.

Looking Back at Learning

As I drive behind the school bus, I can't help but think about my own first day of school. A distant memory now, I vaguely remember walking the ten blocks with my mother, enjoying the sounds and sights that come along with the first day of school. That was decades ago, yet the memory still brings a smile to my face. Schools have been around forever. At some level, school is as old as the human race because people have always been teaching and learning.

Williams Elementary is a fast-growing public school in an area where population growth has outpaced the growth of new schools. A one-story building, it houses an incredible 1,000 children and a complement of administrators, teachers, and support staff. Due to steady county growth, Williams Elementary has added space twice in six years. It amazes me how they continue to teach our children while in a steady state of growth which leads to capacity issues, process challenges, and, at times, outright chaos. I speculate that they must keep their eye on their purpose and deal with each challenge as it arises. After all, the key purpose of a school is to create a place to teach and to learn. If all of us understand this key point and then drive our actions towards that goal, the rest will fall into place.

Thoughts of work creep into my mind… if only organizations could understand that companies are also a place to learn. The fact is that organizations think business is about managing profits, when nothing could be further from the truth. We can't manage profit, as profit is simply the result of revenues minus costs. What we need to do is to understand how we can act upon and influence revenues and costs. Of course profit is an important end goal, but to achieve profitability, we need to focus on the critical variables that result in profit. The most important variable is that the organization needs to continually improve. Continuous improvement is a concept talked about by every organization in business today, yet how many organizations really know what it means to be a culture of continuous improvement? How many companies taking up Lean truly understand what it means to be a Lean Enterprise?

Ah, I think to myself with sudden clarity, a Lean Enterprise is just like Williams Elementary. It is a place to learn and evolve. Just as Williams Elementary produces young, educated minds through learning, a Lean Enterprise will produce profits as a by-product of creating a learning culture of people who continuously improve the organization.

Orlo the Wise Old Owl

... on the Learning Culture

A Lean Enterprise is like a school in that it is a teaching and learning organization. The difference is that the learning is directed toward continuous improvement of how work gets done in order to serve customers better.

All people inside a Lean Enterprise must learn every day. People need to go to work each day with the intent to learn and gain knowledge by relentlessly working to improve the business. This concept is known as **Kaizen** ("kai" rhymes with "sigh"), a Japanese term that means incremental and continuous improvement. To generate improvement, you have to solve problems; to solve problems, you have to learn something you didn't know before. As *you* learn, your organization learns and strengthens.

People learn best and remember better when they are solving problems. Therefore you must create an environment where problems are identified so people can learn and grow while developing solutions to problems.

That's why this kind of endeavor is called a **Lean Journey**, as a *journey* is about the roads you choose to travel and what you learn as you move from destination to destination. Yet while this is a journey, there needs to be an expectation of destinations along the way. Just as we graduate from grade school to high school to college, an organization should know the toll gates they want from their Lean efforts. You need to be able to show how and when Lean will help the business. We call it a journey because excellence does not happen overnight, however there does need to be a time where commitment, hard work, and implementation of Lean will pay off in a measurable and significant way.

And while Lean does need to produce tangible results, a true journey never ends. The Lean Journey is about continuous problem solving, and hence continuous learning. To learn is the essence of life and this holds true for a business organization.

Three Lessons on Learning

- A Lean organization learns through small, incremental improvements
- A Lean organization is not afraid to try new things
- A Lean organization learns from experimentation and making mistakes

Arriving at School

8:45 A.M.

After parking my car, I meet Emilee and Abbey coming off their bus. I can't help but notice that as one bus unloads and drives away, another bus arrives in the roundabout, allowing the buses to flow past the school door. I recall the exact timing for pick-up that had been published in the paper and wonder if all the routes are timed to arrive one after the other.

It makes me think of the disciplined transportation networks I have participated in. It is never easy to design routes that will run on time, every time. There is so much variability inherent in the transportation world that it is virtually impossible to plan for all possible contingencies. However, I have participated on teams that have

successfully developed transportation networks that reliably run on time. I remind myself that nothing can replace careful planning and the *discipline of process* (always thinking in terms of the inputs and steps needed to achieve a desired output).

Emilee gives me a hug and darts off, no longer wanting to be seen with her dad on the first day of school. As a fourth grader, she is clearly beyond the need for parental assistance. Abbey takes my hand in hers and we make our way into the school.

Walking into Williams Elementary on the first day of school is comparable to going into a shopping mall on Christmas Eve. The first thing you feel is sensory overload. I look down at my little Abbey and ask with all sincerity, "What do we do now?"

"I don't know, Daddy. That's why *you're* here!" is Abbey's serious and pointed reply. I can't help but think she reminds me of her mother.

"OK, honey," I say, mentally rolling up my sleeves to take charge of the situation. As I get my bearings amid all the commotion, calm sets in. Slowly and methodically I begin to pick up the visual cues. There are signs with arrows, white boards with lists, and tables with people waiting to help.

Abbey and I walk up to the table labeled "First Graders." After a pleasant conversation with the volunteer parent, we learn that Abbey's first grade class is in room 101. With a map in hand, we follow the arrows and yellow line on the hallway floor toward room 101.

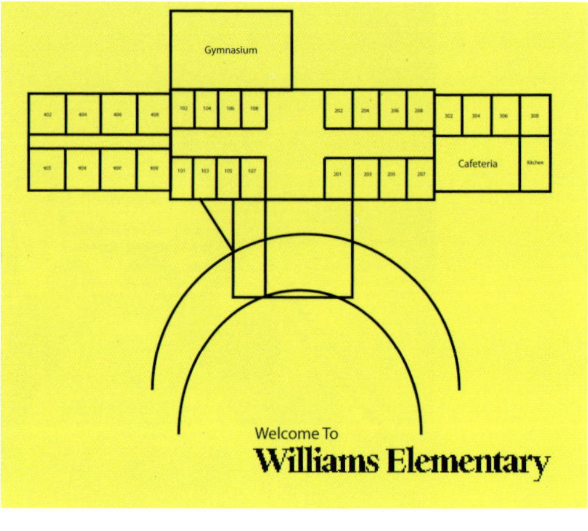

The first grade teacher introduces herself as Ms. Young. It is obvious that she is well prepared for the wide-eyed children streaming into her classroom. It is clear that she has done this before and has carefully worked out an approach to organizing the first day of school. I suspect she knows all too well that without coordination, the situation would fall into chaos.

The closer I look, the more I realize that not only is Ms. Young's procedure thoroughly organized, but so is the entire classroom. Each desk has a nameplate so students know where to sit. Each cubby has a nameplate so students know where to put their lunches, backpacks, and jackets. Along with the numbers 1 to 100, the alphabet is perched at the top of the blackboard. One wall is marked "word wall" and contains important words related to the first week of school. Another wall is prepared to display students' work. A third wall displays name cards in the shape of bumblebees that will show the status of the overall class behavior.

"Ms. Young, this place is incredibly well organized," I compliment her.

"That's one of the signs of an experienced teacher," she says. "We learn quickly that if our classrooms aren't organized, we waste a lot of time trying to figure out what to do." She adds that having an organized classroom lets her give her children a better learning experience, which is especially critical because she teaches first graders who have little previous experience to rely on. "Since I often have 20 to 25 six-year-olds in my classes, everything would quickly descend into chaos if I weren't organized down to every little detail," Ms. Young says. "The children would be confused and feel insecure within minutes."

"Well spoken, Ms. Young," I blurt out with a little too much enthusiasm. I'm thinking about the factories and businesses that want to improve efficiencies, yet their places of business are in chaos. I have often wondered how they can expect to learn and to improve anything when they are in a state of confusion. How in the world do they expect to accomplish anything if their environment is unstable and they are fighting fires all day long?

Ms. Young gives me a polite smile, trying to share my enthusiasm, and then asks me to take a seat at the back of the room so she can call her class to order. The school day is about to begin.

Orlo the Wise Old Owl

... on the Organized Workplace

The Lean Enterprise understands the importance of an organized workplace. A Lean operation must be **stable** and expose problems. To be stable means that you have processes and systems that are predictable and consistent in performance. You cannot be stable if you are always working in and around chaos and clutter. In order to implement Lean concepts, in order to create stability, you must clean up your working area.

The Lean Enterprise creates the organized workplace through the 5 S's:

Sort: Separate and categorize all material and information and discard the unnecessary. (Ms. Young's classroom was organized to feature only the information students would need during the first week of class.)

Set in order: Organize, label, and color-code remaining items for easy use. (Recall the nameplates and tagged cubbyholes in the classroom, which made it easy for students to know where to sit and where to put their belongings.)

Shine: Clean and keep all storage areas void of clutter and unwanted material. (As we'll see later in the day, Ms. Young set up systems so that the students can practice this principle throughout the day.)

Standardize: Create standards for how the workplace should look at all times. (My discussions with Ms. Young showed that she had put a great deal of thought into how her classroom should be organized.)

Sustain: Complete regular audits and improvements to ensure the workplace remains organized. (As I learned, Ms. Young does a self-check at the end of every school day and walks around the classroom putting things back in order. Having regular daily checks is critical for sustainment.)

The 5 S's are the beginning of the Lean Journey and you need to start with an organized workplace. Remember, the goal is to sustain the organized workplace. To clean up once is not the goal. You must create an organized workplace and then maintain its excellence.

Three Lessons on Organizing a Workplace

- Only keep material and information that is critical to the operation
- Have a place for everything and put everything in its place
- Regularly discard all material and information that is not required

Fundamental Principles

9:00 A.M.

Sitting in the back of the class, I notice a sign above Ms. Young's desk, which reads:

"That's an interesting sign," I comment to Ms. Young after she has the children working quietly at their desks. I pause for a moment and then say, "It seems a little old-fashioned, the three R's. I expected something a little more progressive from a modern person like you."

"What do you mean?" she asks, not defensively, but inviting me to say more. The way she asks the question reminds me of the senior coordinators I worked with at Toyota who used the Socratic method of problem solving—asking me a lot of questions until I figured out the answer for myself.

I answer, "Well, in this day and age, there's a lot more to school than reading, writing, and arithmetic. What about science, technology, geography, art, history, and physical education?"

"You're absolutely right," Ms. Young responds. "However, students need basic tools to excel at any of those subjects. They need to master the fundamentals. The three R's are the foundation, the skills and the knowledge, that all learning is built upon."

"I see," I respond. "By focusing on the fundamentals, they'll have success in other areas of study. If they learn to read, write, and master mathematics, it follows that they can learn science, geography, and history."

"That's right, Mr. Robert," Ms. Young says, continuing, "focusing on the fundamentals helps students become more confident. I've often seen that confident students translate their success into other areas, whether academic, athletic, or artistic. I think the term for it is a self-reinforcing loop—success produces confidence, and confidence produces more success."

The basics, I say to myself as I look at the three R's sign and think about what Ms. Young has said. Where and when did business organizations lose sight of the basics? I can feel my blood pressure starting to rise as I once again relive the problems I see when I work with companies trying to improve. Often I find them training employees on advanced mathematical tools when the solution to their problem resides in the basics. Or they spend millions of dollars on technology under the false impression that expensive technology can solve their problems. Usually, the root of the problem is a lack of basic process management. How did we lose our way? How did we get so far out of touch with the basics?

In that instant, I realize my first day of school is going to be a rich learning experience. As they say, "When the student is ready, the teacher appears."

Orlo the Wise Old Owl

... on Getting Back to Fundamentals

The Lean Enterprise focuses on the basics. People will try to complicate the simple and obvious. Do not allow yourself to be tricked into forgetting about the basics. Common sense always prevails.

The Lean Enterprise remembers that business fundamentals are **speed**, **cost**, and **quality**.

- **Speed** is accomplished by eliminating wasteful activities that add meaningless time to a process. The time it takes for something to get through an entire process (**total lead time**) is either **value-added time** or **wasted time** (aka **non-value-added**). Value-added time is any time spent on activities that transform a product or service in ways that customers value and will pay for. Wasted time comprises everything else, including delays, excess transportation, and rework. In almost all processes, value-added time is a mere fraction of total lead time; wasted time is by far the much larger component. So you'll have a much bigger impact on process speed if you focus first on getting rid of non-value-added time.

- **Cost** is reduced by remembering that a business is nothing more than a series of processes. We must eliminate the processes that do not add value in our customers' eyes and that, therefore, serve only to increase our costs.

- **Quality** can be improved if we focus on quality at the source–doing everything possible to make sure that work gets done right the first time, every time, and catching mistakes so they don't turn into customer defects. We must ensure we have quality at the source and that mistakes are not passed down the supply chain.

Before you can focus on speed, cost, and quality, however, you need to emphasize one other fundamental: a respect for people. People want a safe working environment and to be able to use their minds on the job. In my experience, I've seen that solutions to our business problems more often come from the people who live with the problems every day, as opposed to solutions from technology or over-complicated MBA models.

Three Lessons on Fundamentals

- We must treat people with respect and value their opinions
- The fundamentals of business are speed, cost, and quality
- The people who "live" a process every day are best positioned to come up with effective solutions

9:30 A.M.

Setting Expectations

Soon, I find myself wishing I could repeat first grade. It seems like a lot of fun, not to mention giving me more time with Abbey. Ms. Young continues the day with a game where the students walk around the classroom introducing themselves to each other. This activity seems to meet their needs to chat and to move around because when they return to their seats, they settle down quickly.

Ms. Young then shows the students a large bulletin board at the front of the room. "This is our activity board," she announces. "Does anyone recognize those letters across the top row?"

A boy in the third row speaks up. "I think they stand for the days of the week," he says. "That first letter is 'm,' and that's for Monday, isn't it?"

"That's right, Marcus. Very good," says Ms. Young. "Yes, each of those letters represent the days of the week. What's this next letter?" She points to the "T" and continues to go through each letter and the days of the week.

"Now look at the symbols and letters, as they will tell you what we'll be doing each day. Let's look at the plan for Monday. What is this symbol?"

"A plus sign," answer a few of the children.

"Right!" Ms. Young responds. "A plus sign means that we're going to work on math. Can somebody tell me what math is?" The teacher and the students have a discussion about numbers and the advantages of understanding math. She then continues through the rest of the schedule, stopping in turn to talk about each new symbol. I am amazed to hear first graders discussing the importance of learning and the "whys" of learning. In fact, they are learning about learning. In a small way, they have begun their journey toward becoming independent, self-motivated, self-directed learners.

"Since today is the first day of school, we have a very special schedule that I'll talk about in a minute. Tomorrow we will pick up with the regular schedule," says Ms. Young. "What day is tomorrow, class?" There is a chorus of "Thursday." "Tonya, can you come up here and show me which column represents Thursday?" A girl at a back table comes to the front and points out the fourth day of the school week.

"Excellent!" says Ms. Young. "Now let's all try to figure out what we'll be doing tomorrow. Tonya, why don't you stay here and point to a symbol and we'll all call out what it means. Ready?" The students make eye contact with the teacher and then they correctly name each of the activities listed for Thursday.

"Good job, everybody," Ms. Young says encouragingly. "You are very smart." She makes sure that all questions about tomorrow are answered.

She then points out a special schedule she's prepared for the first day of school. "We're going to spend part of our time today on very special activities that don't have symbols. But there are a few that you should recognize. For example, the next symbol is a book. What does a book mean, Carlin?"

"It means reading," said the little boy sitting in front of Ms. Young's desk.

"That's right," Ms. Young says. "We're going to learn to read because reading is one of the best ways to get information. Sometimes I'll read aloud to you, other times you will read aloud to the class or to me, and sometimes you will read silently.

"OK, now it's time to read," she tells the class. "Today, I would like each of you to pick a book from the shelf at the back of the room. Later in the month, we will all go to the school library and you'll have more books to choose from, but for today, you will use the books already in our classroom."

She instructs the children to go to the back of the room in turns, first Tables 1 and 2, then Tables 3 and 4, and then Tables 5 and 6. "Wait until I give the signal to start," she continues. "After you've found a book that you like, take it back to your desk. Look at the pictures. You can learn a lot by looking at pictures. Read the words that you know. If you talk quietly, you may ask a neighbor for help with words that you don't know."

Ms. Young stands at the back of the room and helps the children choose their books. Some read to themselves and others read quietly together. Ms. Young is walking up and down the aisles and when she reaches the back of the room, I compliment her on her teaching techniques.

"I don't think our older daughter's class used an activity board when she was in first grade," I say. "Is that new?"

"Yes and no," she answers. "We've used timetables in different forms and in different ways for years. Having a schedule helps students know what to expect." She explains that they tried out several methods and then settled on this activity board with subject symbols for the younger children. "It helps us to establish an orderly classroom," Ms. Young continues. "Haven't you found that your home runs better when your kids clearly understand your expectations for things like doing homework, bedtime, and chores?"

I agree. "We have a regular schedule during the school week," I say. "That way we avoid a lot of arguments around bedtime and stress in the morning when they wake up."

"We use the same concept to run the classroom," says Ms. Young. "Children feel more secure and learn better when they know what's going on. The more we structure their learning environment, the better they understand their responsibilities. Working within this framework, they know what is expected of them. Their minds are free to concentrate on learning."

"Also," I say to Ms. Young, "I'm impressed with the way you allow the students who can read to help the ones who are just learning. I think people learn better when they work as a team. Everyone is more productive."

"Absolutely," Ms. Young responds. "Everyone knows that the most learning occurs when you have to actually teach something to someone else! So letting our children help each other boosts both their learning and self-confidence."

At that moment, the girl sitting next to Abbey raises her hand and Ms. Young excuses herself to answer a question.

Orlo the Wise Old Owl

... on Making Expectations Clear

To be successful, people need to know where they are and where they are going, as well as how their efforts fit into the greater good of the organization. One of the ways a Lean Enterprise meets these needs and establishes **discipline to the process** is by communicating clear plans that show respect for people and set expectations for what should happen. For people to work at their full potential, they need to know the plan for each day. Not knowing the plan makes them uncomfortable and insecure. No matter where people are in the organizational hierarchy, they will work more efficiently and effectively if expectations are clear.

By having a plan that establishes expectations and communicating the plan, you will have the ability to determine when the plan is not working or when you have veered away from it. Without a plan, or with a plan that isn't clearly communicated to all team members, you will never know for sure just how reality differed from the plan and whether it was because the plan was poor or people didn't know what was expected of them. You need to be able to tell the difference between plan versus actual if you want to take action that will solve the root cause of a problem.

Even something as simple as the activity board that Ms. Young set up helps a great deal, though naturally you should tailor the language and structure to your audience.

A Lean operation is one where problems always become visible. Having a plan and expectations that are clearly communicated to all team members sets the stage for improvement.

Three Lessons on Expectations

- *People will do better in their jobs if they know what is expected of them personally, their work group, and the organization as a whole*
- *Clearly and visually communicate the plan to all team members*
- *Review the plan regularly to assess the actual situation as compared to the plan*

Team Reward — Bumblebee Board

10:15 A.M.

After about 15 minutes of silent reading, the children get a little restless, indicating to their teacher that it is time to put away their books and move on to the next item on the schedule. She instructs the class to close their books and put them away.

Once she has their attention, she explains that she is going to tell them about the Williams' Wizards Award and then they will go to morning recess. She asks, "Does anybody know who Mrs. Wright is?" Only a few hands go up. She calls on my daughter Abbey.

"Mrs. Wright is the principal of the school," Abbey says, pronouncing the word very carefully. "I know because my older sister always calls her that."

"Your sister is correct," Ms. Young answers. "Mrs. Wright is the principal of this school." After a brief discussion with the class about what a principal is, she goes on, "Well, each day for the first month of school, Mrs. Wright will pick one class to win the Williams' Wizards Award for the day."

Hands went up. "What's that?" several children ask.

"The Williams' Wizards Award goes to the class that has done three things well that day," explains Ms. Young.

"First, be nice to each other. [Ms. Young tacks up on the board a sentence strip that reads: 1. Be nice.] The older kids call this being respectful, but I call it being nice. The second rule is to follow school rules. [She tacks a second strip on the board that reads: 2. Follow school rules.] That includes getting ready for each activity, walking quietly in the halls, and behaving in the lunchroom. The third rule is to listen and to learn in class." [A third strip goes up that reads: 3. Listen and learn.]

"Mrs. Wright will pick a class to win the Williams' Wizards Award," explains Ms. Young. "She will announce the winner over the speaker at the end of the day. That class will get its name posted on the Williams' Wizards Award board by the front entrance of the school."

Next, Ms. Young points to the Bumblebee Board and says, "To help us keep track of how well we are doing with our three goals, we have a Team Award – Bumblebee Board. This picture board shows how well we are behaving and how well we are working in class. If we all follow the rules and work hard, we may win the Williams' Wizards Award."

She points to the names written on the bumblebees. "There is a bumblebee card for each of you," she explains. "If you have a difficult time following the rules, your bumblebee card will be turned upside down. If, for example, you are rude, do not follow the rules, or do not do your work, your bumblebee is turned upside down." [Ms. Young demonstrates by turning a card upside down.]

"When someone's bumblebee is turned, they need to work hard to correct the problem. The whole class and I will help the person fix the problem," she says. "We will decide together what must be done. For example, you can correct your bumblebee by reading a story or helping another student. When you have fixed the problem, your bumblebee will be turned right side up. [Ms. Young demonstrates again by returning the name card to the original position.] At the end of the day, if your bumblebee is facing upward, you will get a reward. When all bumblebees are right side up we know that we are learning and playing together successfully. If we try very hard, perhaps one day Mrs. Wright will give us the Williams' Wizards Award."

Ms. Young answers a few questions from the class and then dismisses them for morning recess. I tell Abbey to go ahead with her friends and that I will join her outside in a few minutes.

"Wow," I exclaim a little too loudly, clearly having more fun then I ever imagined I would on my first day of school as a parent. I begin to tell Ms. Young that I can see she's created a classroom that is what we call *self-explaining* in the business world. It allows her and the students to self-examine their progress as individuals and as team members. It is easy to understand, visible to everyone, and problems needing solutions become obvious immediately. I commend her on developing students who are learning to monitor their own learning. They are learning how to organize themselves and how to evaluate based on set expectations. They are learning to know where they stand relative to established standards.

Ms. Young's self-explaining workplace reminds me how organizations on a Lean Journey struggle to make standards clear and visible. Done properly, the visual classroom (or workplace) keeps the "score" out in the open so everyone knows how the group is doing relative to expectations. What is important to know, though, is that the score is not just about win or lose. The score is about showing the actual condition compared to the plan. Plan versus actual is the real score of the game.

"Believe me," Ms. Young says, "children love to know where they stand, to know the score! We grow up knowing that in sports and competitions, the score drives the action. This is healthy competition where individual progress helps the whole group and demonstrates the importance of teamwork. Of course, in a classroom of children, it is important to be sure that individuals who are having difficulty get the appropriate support to maximize their learning styles and to ensure their success. If, for example, over a period of time the same child's bee is always upside down, then appropriate measures would be taken to provide extra support for that student."

"You are so right," I agree with Ms. Young. "In school and in our workplace, we need to know our people and to know the score of the game. How else can we know what and where we need to improve?"

Orlo the Wise Old Owl

... on the Self-Explaining Workplace

When the Lean Enterprise focuses on visual management and the 5 S's, the self-explaining workplace develops over time. This is critical because people want to know the score of the game they are playing. People want to know what standards they are being held to.

Standardization and standard work are critical to continuous improvement because standards provide the baseline against which we judge the impact of change. Without standards, we have no basis for evaluating whether process changes are true improvements. Is one procedure better than another? Are materials from one supplier better than those from another? You can make a valid judgment about improvement only if you have a baseline for what the process was like before and after a change.

Consequently, the foundation of continuous improvement is standardization. But don't think this means that processes never change in a Lean Enterprise. In fact, the reverse is true: one of the Lean paradoxes is that standards must change as often as required to improve the business. The trick is that you always replace one standard with a new, improved standard that is proven to produce better results.

As either a leader or team member, when you walk into an operation, you want to know instantly whether the operation is ahead or behind or right on schedule for the day. The self-explaining workplace allows managers and team members to prioritize and focus on the areas that need attention at that moment. Whether in the factory, the warehouse, or the office, you need to understand instantly what is happening in the operation. The whole team needs to know if anything is out of order so you can fix potential problems before they become real problems. This helps to ensure you are working on the right things at the right time. Working on the right things at the right time is what creates an efficient and effective organization.

Creating a self-explaining workplace is challenging. You need to visually show the score that represents your standards and measures of success. This isn't always easy. You need to define and make visible those measures that tell you in an instant about the health and status of the process relative to the plan.

Three Lessons on a Self-Explaining Workplace

- "See in an instant" by using visual methods to show how your operation is currently running
- Understand, review, and analyze the current condition as a team
- Act as a team when the visual cues indicate there is a problem

Shared Reading & Henry Ford

10:45 A.M.

When the kids return from recess, they are red-faced and smiling. I remember that feeling; exercise and fresh air induce a happy and relaxed feeling that, in turn, makes us better learners. Again, the children easily find their seats using their nameplates.

Ms. Young announces to her students that it is time to do shared reading.

"What's shared reading?" Abbey asks.

"Great question, Abbey," Ms. Young replies. "Shared reading is when we learn to read together using books, stories, and songs. Today we will read the words to a song and sing them together. Don't worry if you do not know all of the words because we will be singing aloud together. So just do the best that you can. I will sing first and you will listen and then we will sing together. We will learn from each other."

This is a creative and fun way to learn to read. The chorus of voices provides a safety net for children who are unable to read fluently by themselves. Here is my chance to stop thinking about work and to have fun. Using the overhead projector, the teacher displays the song we are about to sing.

I literally fall off my chair! (Fortunately for me the chairs in first grade are built low to the ground.) The song that has appeared on the screen is about Henry Ford.

“The song we are going to sing today,” Ms. Young says, “is about Henry Ford. Does anybody know who Henry Ford was?” A little boy immediately throws his hand in the air. “Yes, Ryan,” Ms. Young responds.

“He’s the man who built my daddy’s pick-up truck,” Ryan answers with complete confidence.

“That’s right, Ryan,” Ms. Young explains. “In fact, he is the person who helped to start the automobile industry more than 100 years ago. He is a famous inventor and engineer and that’s why we are going to learn about him.”

At this point, I am so excited, I can hardly contain myself. I want to jump up, go to the chalkboard, and start teaching the students about Henry Ford. I want to tell them about how Henry Ford understood and worked to perfect the idea of interchangeable and standard parts.

Once Mr. Ford engineered standard parts that would fit together with other standard parts, he was able to create the assembly line by setting up workstations along the line, with material being delivered to the workers at each station. This allowed the automobiles to flow steadily through the manufacturing process one operation at a time (what we now think of as “flow production”).

I want to tell the students that Henry Ford was one of the first Lean manufacturers and how he was committed to lead time reduction through the elimination of waste (any activity that does not add value for the customer). Mr. Ford understood the power of lead time reduction and that is why he only wanted to build the Model T in black: one model, one color. Adding more models or more colors would add complexity to the supply chain, which would slow down the process and increase overall customer-order-to-delivery lead time.

I want to tell the eager students how Henry Ford was a mass producer and how this is very different than a batch producer. A mass producer is somebody that builds a lot of product in total, but a batch producer is one who believes that you should build in big batches in order to take advantage of perceived economies of scale. But we know economies of scale do not produce cost savings if the result is that we build big batches of inventory that will never sell.

I am jolted from my daydream by their singing. Ms. Young is guiding the children through the words to the song. I follow along, enjoying the sound of their voices. The tune is a catchy one and before I know what is happening, I am singing along with the class. The song goes like this:

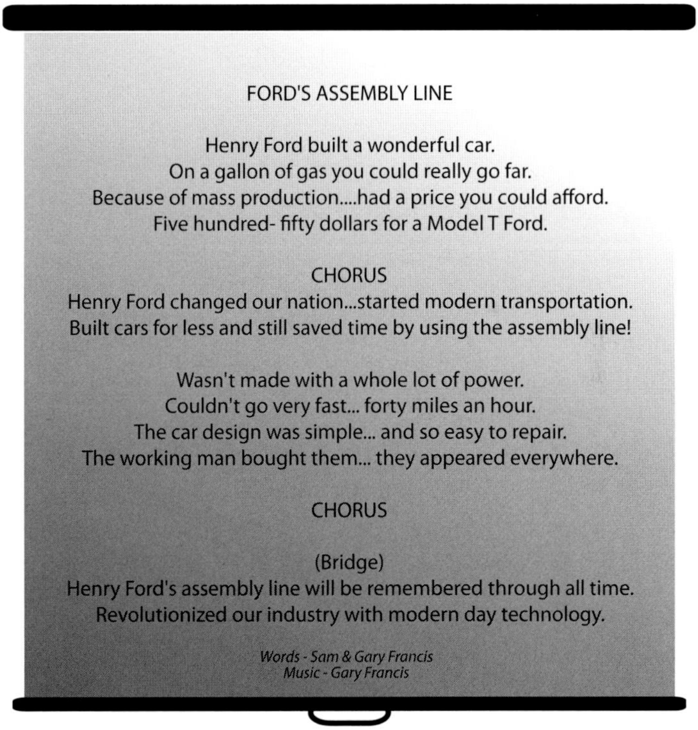

The lyrics of this song about Henry Ford are like words from my heart because they embrace concepts like saving time, low price, assembly lines, and simple design. My head is spinning while I listen to Ms. Young talk to her class about the song.

"Does anybody know what an assembly line is?" she asks the class. Seven students raise their hands immediately. In fact, the hands are up before Ms. Young can finish the question. She calls on Peter.

"Umm," Peter says, "an assembly line is, umm, umm."

I smile to myself as Peter tries in vain to come up with an answer. I expect he has heard this term and he thinks he knows what it is, but can't quite come up with the words. Then again, I've noticed how children will raise their hands to answer a question before they have given the topic a thought or even listened to the question.

"Can anyone tell me what an assembly line is?" Ms. Young asks again. Showing some restraint this time, no student raises his or her hand. So Ms. Young turns to me. "Mr. Robert, would you like to tell us about an assembly line?"

I jump to attention. Would I? I am bursting with ideas to share. Thinking ahead I say, "I certainly can, Ms. Young. In fact, if it is alright with you, I can show the class how an assembly line works. A picture is worth a thousand words, but actually doing something is worth a million pictures!" Ms. Young gives me a smile of approval and I spring into action.

I set up an assembly line to build paper airplanes. Grabbing some paper from the cabinet I spend the next 10 minutes organizing the children into an assembly line. Together we determine there are 12 steps in building a paper airplane. We have 24 students, so I set up two assembly lines so everybody can participate. It is interesting to see how quickly the class discovers bottlenecks in their assembly lines. Several students get frustrated and start to yell at their classmates to speed up or slow down depending on where they are in the line. I am witnessing classic organizational behavior: each first grader is absorbed in trying to perfect their own station and annoyed with those whose stations are not running smoothly.

When we finish building our airplanes, I ask Ms. Young if I can tell the students more about Henry Ford. “Of course, Mr. Robert,” she replies. “We would never miss an opportunity to learn.” Abbey is giving me that “please don't embarrass me, Daddy” look.

I spend the next 10 minutes telling the class about Henry Ford and his contributions to Lean manufacturing. I talk about mass production as opposed to batch production and I talk about the importance of lead time reduction. By the time I start introducing the topics of product and supply chain complexity, Ms. Young realizes that the children have reached their saturation point and politely interrupts. With Ms. Young's interruption of my lecture, I look to Abbey, who is giving me the “Daddy, I really love you, but you did it again” look.

Orlo the Wise Old Owl

... on Henry Ford & the Lean Enterprise

The idea of the Lean Enterprise has been around for a long time. It is not simply a new *program* that organizations will embrace for a few months. It is a *way of thinking.*

The focus of Lean thinking is always on the elimination of waste. In fact, the Lean Enterprise defines eight categories of waste that do not add value to any organization. These wastes are:

1) **Overproduction**: Building or buying more than we need or earlier than we need

2) **Inventory**: Anything that we spend money on—supplies, materials, facilities, equipment, information, people—to hide the flaws in a process (see discussion below)

3) **Correction**: Doing things over because they were not done right the first time

4) **Overprocessing**: Doing more than is required to meet customer needs

5) **Motion**: All motion that does not add value to the product or process

6) **Waiting**: All things that cause waiting or hinder our work

7) **Transportation**: Transportation in excess of what is required, if perfect one-piece flow existed

8) **Human Intellect**: Missed ideas by not engaging the people who do the work

The issue of inventory as a type of waste usually needs special attention. To draw an analogy, picture your organization as a boat navigating down a river. The river represents the business environment. Just below the water are many rocks. These rocks represent the wastes described above. Building on the analogy, inventory is the water level of the river. As inventory goes up, so does the water level.

As we flow down the river, we are very cognizant of the rocks (waste) below. When we see a rock, we can do one of three things.

1. Try to navigate around the rocks—the equivalent of fire fighting each and every day.

2. Raise the water level (inventory level) in order to ensure the river flows on top of the rocks.

3. Eliminate the rocks permanently, making the river void of waste and problems.

We cannot simply continue to throw resources and inventory at our problems! The goal of the Lean Enterprise is to expose problems and eliminate them. So while many organizations hide their problems with inventory, the Lean Enterprise works to expose them! This can only be done by lowering the water level; we must reduce inventories in order to expose waste and problems and then we must eliminate the waste once and for all.

Three Lessons on Flow

- Henry Ford's basic idea of "flow production" (where work flows steadily through a process and materials/information are delivered as needed to workstations) is still sound
- Lean is not just another program of the month; it is a way of thinking
- Lean is about the elimination of anything that makes us waste our time or resources

One at a Time

11:15 A.M.

Along with their teacher, the students look at the activity board to figure out the subject of their next lesson. The symbol "+" indicates mathematics is next.

Like everything else in first grade, the mathematics lesson intrigues me. I completed my undergraduate degree in mathematics. A shiver goes through me as I relive my struggle to successfully complete vector calculus, complex variables, and differential equations. Reminiscing about my student days reminds me of my most valued professor, Dr. Gerry, an amazing leader and teacher. I remember him taking the time to go over my questions and challenges. He wouldn't just give me the answer, but rather would ask me questions until I discovered the answer for myself. I smile now as I remember how, years later, when I completed my MBA, Dr. Gerry drove a long distance to attend my graduation.

Fortunately for the first grade students, Ms. Young is not teaching vector calculus—she is teaching the basics, simple addition and subtraction.

After teaching a lesson in subtraction, Ms. Young directs her class to a short arithmetic exercise, printed on the blackboard. This gives them an opportunity to practice the concept that she just taught. "Now," she says, "before you start your board work, I want to review the restroom routine. Lunch will be in about 15 minutes.

"We need to wash our hands each day before we eat lunch," she begins. "Who can tell me why we do this?" A mini health lesson and discussion follows. The children share previously learned information about the importance of hand washing to kill germs. She tells them that they will go to the restroom one at a time, starting with Table 1 and continuing through Table 6.

At this point, my little Abbey raises her hand and asks, "Ms. Young, we have four people at our table. How do we know who should go first?" I am proud of her question. Though she's only six years old, it is clear to me that she is absorbing my conversations at home about the importance of disciplined processes.

"Great question, Abbey," Ms. Young replies. "Since we're learning to solve problems through talking and working together as a team, I'm going to ask each table to take a few minutes to make a plan for using the restroom. Talk about who will go first, then second, third, and fourth at your table. Then I want you all to be ready to share your plans with the class. You have four minutes. I will ring the bell when your time is up."

Ms. Young walks around the classroom answering questions, stopping to listen and to help or to redirect the conversation at the tables, if necessary. After four minutes, she rings the bell. Then she asks one

person from each table to explain their plan. By the end of this discussion, all students seem to understand and accept the routine. At the teacher's go-ahead nod, the first child from Table 1 proceeds to the restroom down the hall while the other children begin their arithmetic practice exercise from the blackboard.

Once again, I just have to quiz Ms. Young about her methods. "Why do you do the restroom routine this way?" I ask.

"Well, Mr. Robert," she replies, "I used to have the entire class line up to go to the restroom, but I soon found that it took a long time and that the students waiting in line got restless and misbehaved. The children who finished early ended up just sitting at their desks waiting for instructions. All in all, I lost a lot of precious teaching time, which is unacceptable."

She adds that, with the new method, the children go to the restroom one at a time while everyone else spends the time learning. "As you can see, no children are just sitting, waiting at their desks. And no children are waiting in line," she says. "They are doing their work, except for the brief moments they spend in the restroom washing their hands."

"One-piece flow!" I exclaim.

"Pardon me?" Ms. Young responds, obviously a little taken aback by my enthusiasm.

"Well," I begin to explain, "in business, we teach organizations that they need to focus on one-piece flow. The idea is to keep inventories, material, and information moving along at a steady flow toward the customer. Any time material or information stops, the waste of waiting occurs, costs increase, and the customer suffers."

"Interesting," Ms. Young says with sincerity.

She then leaves to answer a question from one of the children as I ponder why more companies don't move to one-piece flow. It's not just a million dollar question—for some companies, it is a multi-million dollar question.

One-piece flow may seem logical to me, but many people find it is counterintuitive. People in business have been trained to think of "economies of scale," so they think that moving big batches of material and information is better. Unfortunately, any gains they may get through economies of scale are generally offset by the waste of having to move and store big batches of inventory. Companies that work in big batches often end up making a big batch of something that the customer has not ordered and does not want. That is the waste of overproduction, which is considered the worst waste because of its many ripple effects: overproduction creates many other wastes.

To make matters worse, while the company is making the *unwanted* items, the customer could be waiting for delivery of a *wanted* order that hasn't been filled. By the time the company switches to producing what is in demand, they have huge stockpiles of materials or products that customers don't want but that the company has to pay to move around and store.

Wishing I had an interested listener, I look around for a whiteboard to draw it out. But my attention is diverted by seeing that Ms. Young has recognized an escalating situation in the classroom and is rushing off to Table 6 to mediate.

Orlo the Wise Old Owl

... on One-Piece Flow

The Lean Enterprise does not focus on big-batch thinking or economies of scale. Lean operations focus on one-piece flow, which means that all materials and information flow steadily toward the end of the process (and ultimately the customer) without stopping. In Ms. Young's class, she set up a system where there was a steady flow of children into and out of the restrooms, which minimized the disruption and allowed the whole class to spend more time learning.

One-piece flow will not happen if we are batch thinkers. Building batches means that material and information must wait while the batch is being made, stored, and then slowly used up. Waiting is a pure waste of time and money.

One-piece flow reduces process lead time (you get from order to delivery much more quickly), reduces inventories (which reduces costs), and makes problems more visible when they arise. One-piece flow also allows us to be flexible when dealing with changes in the marketplace. To be flexible means having the ability to change when

the customer's needs change. If you do not change with the customer, then you will build items you don't need, which may become obsolete and result in waste. This is overproduction, the worst waste of all.

Implementing one-piece flow will be challenging for companies conditioned to think in terms of big batches. They must overcome this thinking and look at flow in a very different way. One-piece flow will produce greater results for the organization than any gains made through perceived economies of scale.

Three Lessons on One-Piece Flow

- One-piece flow means that materials and information do not stop on the way to the customer
- To implement one-piece flow, you must rethink your paradigm around economies of scale
- One-piece flow will make problems visible, allowing you to problem solve and learn more quickly

11:50 A.M.

The Class Solves a Problem

The restroom process has come to a grinding halt. I focus on the situation and realize that the process has stopped at the last group, Table 6. So five of the six groups successfully implemented their plan. Now, however, two stressed-looking little kids both believe it is their turn to wash their hands. Ms. Young arrives just in time to intervene.

"What's going on?" she asks all four kids at the table, not just Lisa and Brian, who are evidently having the dispute. The two children start pleading their case to Ms. Young at the same time. They're both talking and not listening to each other or to the teacher. It is chaotic. I can't make any sense of the conversation.

Ms. Young speaks respectfully as she calms everyone down. "OK," she says, "we can't solve the problem until we are calm and ready to listen. So let's all take a few deep breaths and relax our shoulders." She demonstrates for the students, and gets the whole class involved in deep breathing.

"Now, I will ask the class to join us on the carpet for a short meeting to do some problem solving." The students move onto the carpet and sit in a circle. Ms. Young sits between Brian and Lisa, who are calming down but are obviously still upset.

"We need to work through this problem as a team," Ms. Young continues in a quiet voice. "Obviously, there's some misunderstanding about the plan for leaving the room at Table 6. I know that, as a class, you're going to be very good at solving this problem since 20 of you have successfully worked through your own plan. Now, what were we trying to do?"

A student answers, "The plan was to leave the room and to go to the restroom one at a time when our turn came."

"Very good," Ms. Young says in a very complimentary way. Then she directs a request at the students from Table 6. "In turn, I want each of you to tell us about your plan and why you think it didn't work."

Brian speaks first, "When it came to our table, I wanted to go first but Lisa cut in front of me. It wasn't fair, so I got up at the same time as her and then we started fighting."

"Very good, Brian," Ms. Young speaks in the same complimentary tone. "So the plan was to go one at a time, but the actual situation was that you tried to go two at a time." The four faces from Table 6 nod at Ms. Young in agreement.

"Well done," Ms. Young goes on. "Now that we know the problem, we need to ask ourselves why it happened." At this point, both Lisa and Brian are settling down. I wonder if it's because they understand that they are being treated fairly.

Ms. Young asks Brian the next question. "Brian, why did this problem happen?" Brian thinks for a minute and then answers. "Because Lisa got up when it was my turn to go!"

Ms. Young turns to the little girl. "Lisa," she asks, "why did you get up at the same time as Brian?"

"Because I thought it was my turn to go," Lisa answers.

Ms. Young continues speaking with Lisa. "*Why* did you think it was your turn to go?" Lisa's brows furrow as she tries to remember and before she can answer, Jimmy, who also sits at Table 6, jumps into the conversation. Sounding a little nervous, he says, "Our table didn't know how to decide who would go first. Then when it was our turn, Lisa and Brian both jumped up because they thought it was their turn."

"Very good, Jimmy," Ms. Young compliments him. "So the real problem is that your table did not have a complete plan to decide who would go first?" The four children from Table 6 look at each other, then nod in agreement. Ms. Young has found the root cause of the problem.

"Great," Ms. Young continues. "Now that we know the reason for the problem, we need to find a solution." Smiling faces nod in agreement. Even Lisa and Brian look pleased. "Here's a thought," Ms. Young says to the whole class. "Let's share our ideas." When the students agree, Ms. Young asks students from other groups to explain how they chose who would go first. Some groups decided to go clockwise around their table, starting with the child closest to the door. Some did the equivalent of drawing straws. Table 6, with the help of the class, makes a better plan that seems to satisfy each of them.

I am impressed. The students return to their seats to finish the math practice and Table 6 begins acting on its new plan. I turn to Ms. Young and say, "Ms. Young, this is incredible!"

"How so, Mr. Robert?" she asks, answering with a question once again.

"Well," I say, "you helped Brian and Lisa understand the root cause of the problem and they got ideas for solutions from the entire class. You used the '5 Whys' for root cause analysis and then you got the students to share best practices."

"I'm not sure about all those terms," Ms. Young tells me, "but I do know there is no better way to learn than by solving problems. My goal is to create a teaching and learning environment where my students are comfortable, relaxed, and ready to learn together through problem solving."

I am about to tell Ms. Young that organizations also need basic problem-solving skills, but all of her students are back from the restroom and it is time to go to lunch.

Orlo the Wise Old Owl

... on Problem Solving

The Lean Enterprise is a problem-solving culture. To become Lean means that all people in the organization are focused on identifying the root causes of problems and eliminating those causes. In the Lean Enterprise, having "no problem" is a problem because it means people aren't paying attention. Every process has and will continue to have problems. You need to give people the tools and freedom to expose and fix those problems. This will be tough on the organization in the beginning, as many managers believe their job is to hide problems. In a Lean Enterprise, finding problems is good! Hiding problems is bad!

Once problems are exposed, you need to fix the root cause. Don't fall into the trap of simply fixing the symptoms that have appeared as a result of the problem. Fixing symptoms results in a temporary fix at best. Fixing the root cause will eliminate it entirely.

A simple technique for forcing you to dive down to find the root cause of a problem is to keep asking "why" until it doesn't make sense to ask "why" any more. In our classroom case, Ms. Young asked the students "why" there was an argument at Table 6. The answer was that two students got up at the same time to use the restroom. She asked "why" a second time–why did Lisa get up at the same time as Brian? The answer was that Lisa thought it was her turn. Ms. Young asked "why" a third time–why did Lisa think it was her turn? The answer was that the table didn't really have a plan to decide who would go first. The solution was therefore to have a better plan.

So in this case, it took three "whys" to expose a root cause that was "actionable." Sometimes it will take more; other times less (the rule-of-thumb is "5 Whys"). The point is that eventually you will know the real reason why a problem exists and can find a solution that will remove the problem permanently.

The Lean Enterprise finds solutions to problems through sharing of best practices. Known as **Yokoten** (pronounced yoh-koh-ten), this is the art of sharing knowledge across an organization. Sharing knowledge and ultimately creating a learning culture is the overarching essence of the Lean Enterprise.

Three Lessons on Problem Solving

- Lean is about exposing problems and solving them at the root cause through knowledge sharing
- You can get to the root cause of a problem by asking "why" multiple times
- Once you've exposed the root cause, you can develop a more effective solution to the problem

Lunch in the Cafeteria

12:02 P.M.

Ms. Young looks at the clock on the wall and then at the watch on her wrist. Confirming the two timepieces are in sync, she looks down at her students and announces, "Twelve-o-two, time for lunch."

I watch my Abbey get up and retrieve her lunch box from her cubby, finding it interesting that she clearly remembers the lunch procedures learned in kindergarten, where she attended half days. Obviously she paid attention to daily routines and standard procedures and did not forget how things worked over summer vacation.

Ms. Young has the class line up in single file inside the classroom and, checking her watch again, leads the brigade of young minds out of the classroom, down the hall, and toward the cafeteria.

Breaking rank, I walk beside her, commenting, "Ms. Young, you seem very punctual about this lunch process."

"What do you mean, Mr. Robert?" she asks.

"Well, I noticed you looking at the clock on the wall and your watch several times before escorting the students down to the cafeteria."

"We have to be punctual, Mr. Robert," Ms. Young says. "The lunch process is extremely disciplined because we have 1,000 students in this school and they all need to eat lunch. Arriving at the cafeteria exactly on time and keeping to the schedule is critical."

I give her a smile and respond, "I see. You have a lot of children to get through a process quickly, so you have to be careful in the planning and execution."

"Right," says Ms. Young. "We could never feed all 1,000 students at the same time. Our cafeteria is small, so students would spend their whole lunch break waiting in line."

I begin to wonder if schools face the same challenges and constraints as business organizations. I often run into situations where resources are overburdened, where the flow of work is uneven (heavy at some times, light at others), and where processes seem to have a lot of built-in waiting time (which isn't good for the company or its customers!).

Walking into the Williams Elementary cafeteria, I am struck by two initial thoughts. The first is how small the cafeteria really is and the second is how fast the line is moving. Students seem to be flowing smoothly through the process of picking up their trays, choosing their food, and paying at the register.

I expect to stand in line with Abbey, but there is no "standing." We move through the line one-by-one, with a rhythmic and steady beat. Everything seems calm and well-ordered. Unable to fight my natural tendencies, I make a mental note of the process and conclude that it goes like this:

Step 1: Help yourself to an empty tray

Step 2: Help yourself to a carton of milk, choosing between chocolate and white

Step 3: Ask a cafeteria server for your food, choosing between three different items

Step 4: Pay one of two cashiers waiting to help the students (each student puts a password into a handheld keypad to initiate a payment from a lunch credit account)

Sailing through the process, Abbey and I go to a table in the open area of the cafeteria. Unfortunately, the chairs and tables are not built for adults and it is hard for me to get my legs under the table, so I am forced to sit with my legs in the aisle. Abbey starts having "little girl" chats with her friends, so I excuse myself to investigate the cafeteria process. Squeezing through the students, trying to get to the front of the line to see better, I come face-to-face with a "take charge" type of man standing in the kitchen area.

"Don't disrupt the line," he cautions me, "you will disturb the beat."

"Sorry," I say, trying to befriend the boss of this operation. "I'm fascinated with the flow of your process. This is remarkably efficient."

Sizing me up and deciding I am not a threat to his operation, he says, "Well, step back here and get out of the line. You are upsetting the beat!"

We introduce ourselves. I learn that Mr. Brunt has been running the Williams Elementary cafeteria since his retirement from an automotive component manufacturing company. His children are grown and he enjoys his part-time position.

"Just call me Bud, like everyone else around here does," he says.

"OK, Bud," I comply, wanting to be on his good side.

"So," Bud responds, "what do you want to know about this process?"

"I am a student of Lean, Bud," I say. "I'm visiting the school today with my daughter Abbey, who just started first grade. It seems to me like you've structured this cafeteria process just like you would a manufacturing line in that automotive company you just mentioned. I'm presuming that by 'the beat,' you mean the pace at which this process operates."

"Right you are," Bud replies. "The beat is the beat of these students. It's the rhythm of this process. I have to get one classroom through the process every 3.75 minutes and one student every 9 seconds. That's the beat of my operation and I try not to let anything get in the way of that beat."

My jaw drops to the floor. "Takt Time," I say to Bud. "You are running your operation to Takt Time!"

Bud smiles. I can't help but think that I have just made his day. "Takt" is a German word for drumbeat; it represents the beat of customer demand and is well known in the manufacturing industry. In other words, all operations should be working to produce output (parts, products, services) at the Takt rate.

"I used to call it Takt Time, but that was before. Now I just call it the 'beat,'" Bud replies. "Want to see how I came up with the beat?"

"Do I?" I reply. "I can't wait!"

We walk behind the two cash registers and on the back wall, in plain sight, is a whiteboard with the basic math written on it with a black marker.

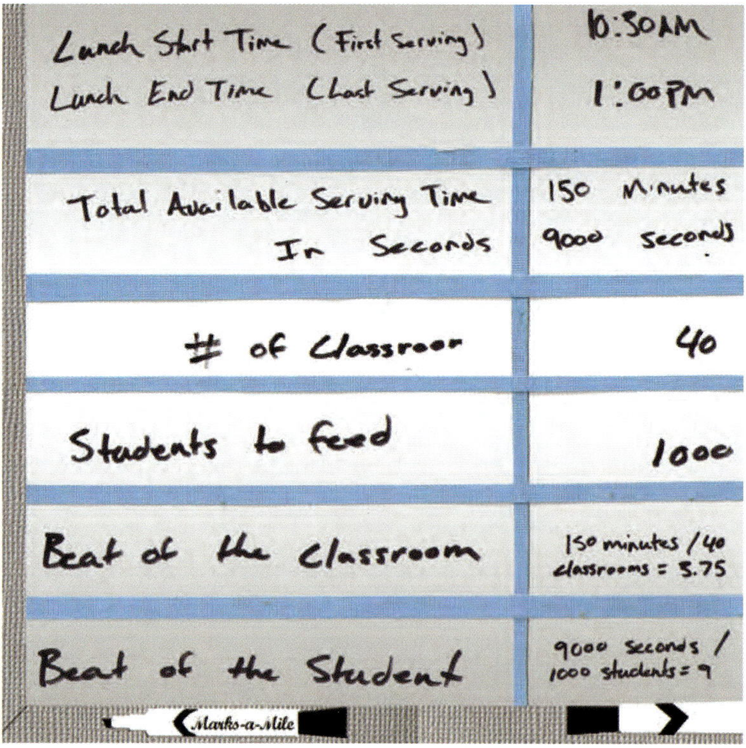

Bud starts to explain his logic. "I know I have only 150 minutes to feed these children. I also know I have 40 classrooms. So if I divide 150 by 40, I need to feed one classroom every 3.75 minutes. I also know that, in total, I have 1,000 students to feed. If I divide 150 minutes by 1,000, I learn that I need to feed one child every 9 seconds. In other words, the beat is 9 seconds."

"*Wow!*" I say, completely and sincerely amazed.

Bud explains, "Once I know the beat is 9 seconds, I design each step in the process to be completed in 9 seconds. That way, the children just march to the beat of the 9-second drummer."

"I imagine that it doesn't always work out that each step takes 9 seconds," I say.

Bud frowns at me and replies, "Unfortunately not. That was a challenge. Take, for example, the cash register where the kids enter their code to pay for lunch. I learned that the average student takes 18 seconds to punch their code in and move along. That led to a bottleneck—students standing in line waiting for others to enter their codes. At first, I tried to teach the children to do the routine faster, but I just could not get to a consistent time of 9 seconds. So, I added another cash register, which meant we could have two children punching in their codes at the same time. That got me the 9-second beat."

"But you had the expense of buying a second cash register," I point out.

"Right," says Bud, "but our only other option would have been to extend the lunch hours. We would have had kids in here practically the whole day! And some of them would have been eating lunch at nine o'clock, with others having to starve until two or even three o'clock."

He points out that knowing what the beat needs to be allows him to do better planning—having the right number of employees to staff the line, buying the right amount of food, knowing exactly when to move more food from the freezer to the shelves. "The beat is everything!" he concludes.

I start to ask another question, but Bud looks at his watch and informs me it is time for me to move along so he can focus on his operation.

Orlo the Wise Old Owl

... on Takt Time

The Lean Enterprise knows that everything starts and ends with the customer. To get high quality, you must know the customer's expectations and perception of your products/services. To control costs, you must also know the rhythm of customer demand for each product or service. Remember, overproduction is the worst waste. You can eliminate overproduction if you focus on **process flow** and the **pace** of work–that's how to produce exactly to the rhythm of customer demand.

The fulfillment stream and supply chain are like a dance. You must dance to the beat of the customer. Once you know the customer-demand rhythm, all organizational processes in the entire fulfillment stream need to be designed to dance to that same rhythm. This beat is known as **Takt Time**. As noted in the story, "takt" is a German word that roughly means "drumbeat."

Takt Time is different than process time. Process time is simply how long it takes to complete a task or process. Takt Time is the number of times you need to complete the task in any given time period in order to fulfill the customer's need. For example, in Bud's cafeteria, it would take the students about three minutes to pick out and pay for their food (that's the process time), but Bud had the process arranged so that one student could be done every 9 seconds (that's the Takt Time). As Bud demonstrated, you calculate Takt Time by determining how much time is available (he had 9,000 seconds) and the demand quantity (1,000 students).

If every process in the system had a process time that was equal to Takt Time, then you would have perfect one-piece flow. This is the ultimate goal of the Lean Enterprise.

Three Lessons on Takt Time

- Takt Time is the rhythm or beat of actual customer demand
- Takt Time is calculated by dividing "available working time" by "demand quantity"
- The goal is to establish a beat where an output is generated exactly when it is demanded by the customer

1:00 P.M.

Afternoon Set Up

It is a nice day, so Abbey's class goes outside to play after lunch. Ms. Young asks me to come back a few minutes early to help her with the set up for the afternoon activities. She says, "As I explained this morning, I find that the classroom runs better when I set up ahead of time. I can do it myself, but…"

"I'd be happy to help," I say. "I'm glad to be doing something useful."

I join Ms. Young in the classroom before the bell rings to summon the students from the playground. She is distributing stickers of firefighters and police officers, alternating so that there are two of each type of sticker at each table of four students.

"What are those stickers for?" I ask.

"You'll see," says Ms. Young. "I'll let you be just as surprised as the students. In the meantime, please pass out those papers from my desk and put one sheet by each student's chair."

Ever the obedient first grader, I promptly perform the task. She then has me distribute boxes of colored pencils. Just as we finish, the school bell rings and soon the students file back into the room. Ms. Young observes as the students find their assigned seats and then calls the class to order by clapping out a simple snap-and-clap pattern, which the students repeat.

Once she has the attention of all the students, she says, "We're going to do some drawing in a minute, but first, look at the stickers on the tables. Who can tell me what these people do?" The students share their ideas about police officers and firefighters. "Now I want you to pick up the sticker in front of your chair, take off the backing, and put the sticker on your shirt."

She waits as the students comply. "That's great, everyone. For this afternoon, you will be working with a partner. Each police officer, please pick one of the firefighters at your table to be your partner." Again, a pause as the students complete the task.

"Does everyone have a partner?" Ms. Young asks. "Well done, class. Now I want each of you to draw a picture. Since I want to learn more about all of you—and we all want to learn more about each other—you could draw a picture of yourself doing something that you like to do. It could be a hobby or an activity that you enjoy. It could be something that you do all the time or something that you did this summer. This is my picture." Ms. Young holds up a picture that she has drawn of herself gardening, then continues, "I drew myself in my garden because that is something that I like to do in the summer. There is paper and colored pencils on each table for you to use. Are there any questions?"

A few students ask questions and then the class gets to work. Ms. Young walks around the room, encouraging students to draw and answering questions. When most of the students are finished drawing, she gives further instructions.

"Let me see who the police officers are," she says. Hands are raised. "I want each police officer to tell their partner about their picture. You will have four minutes. When I ring the bell [Ms. Young demonstrates ringing the bell] the firefighters will then have their turn to talk about their pictures."

The noise level increases as each pair of students discusses their pictures. When both partners have had a chance to tell their stories, Ms. Young asks for volunteers to come forward and to share their pictures with the whole class. When there are no more volunteers, Ms. Young praises the students, saying, "You have done a fine job. In a minute, I will have you put your pictures in your cubbyholes so you can take them home this afternoon to show your parents. But first, would the police officers from Table 1 and Table 6 please collect the colored pencils and bring them up to my desk? Thank you."

While this task is being completed Ms. Young tells the students that they have time to choose an activity from one of the learning centers. She tells them to put their pictures away then go to the activity tables to pick out an activity. She asks the firefighters to go first. She says to the police officers, "When your partner returns to your table, it will be your turn to go and choose an activity."

There is a momentary rumble as the students move around each other. I am surprised, though, at how quickly everything comes back to order. The tables are cleared off, the pencils put away, and each student has chosen an activity. She has transitioned the students to a new activity without interrupting the flow of the afternoon in any way.

During this quiet time, I ask Ms. Young to tell me more about the use of the police officer and the firefighter stickers. "Your afternoon set-up worked very well, Ms. Young," I say. "I think I know some of the answers, but why did you use police officer and firefighter stickers?"

"I chose those stickers in part because they will help me introduce a unit we will be doing on Community Helpers," she continues. "From the students' point of view, the stickers are fun. The stickers catch the students' attention, so they are motivational. From my point of view, I include them as part of my set-up because they make it easier for me to give instructions and divide the group into partners quickly."

"Why do you have the students work with partners sometimes?" I ask.

Ms. Young replies, "At the end of the day, a teacher's biggest challenge is to ensure that her class spends as much time as possible learning. We recognize that some things we do take away from that time. There are routines and activities that are a necessary part of school but that don't help the students learn. At this school, we make it a practice to look at those things that take away from our teaching time and get rid of as much of them as we can. We want to enrich the minds of our children in every way that we can."

She pauses to look around the room, then continues. "Every teacher knows that moving from one subject or activity to another can take up a lot of time because students can easily get confused," she explains. "Using the stickers lets me spell out some simple procedures for moving on to the next activity, and it lets me double up on the activity in the classroom by assigning different tasks to the firefighters and police officers."

"As you saw, we got through the switch from the drawing activity to individual activities very quickly—which gives the students more time for learning," she concludes.

For the third time that morning, I'm stopped in my tracks by what I'm hearing. "Ms. Young," I say, "you're talking about the difference between value-added processes and non-value-added processes! You're also talking about reducing set up times in order to continually be doing value-added activities!"

"Once again, I don't quite know the terms you use," says Ms. Young, "but as a group, the teachers routinely discuss a typical day for a child to see how much of it is valuable and how much is not valuable from the teaching and learning perspective. I'm guessing that's what you mean by value-added and non-value-added time."

"Exactly!" I reply. "What do you learn from those discussions with other teachers?"

"One of the most valuable parts is simply defining exactly what happens to students during the course of any given school day," she answers. "But we also look at the issue we were just talking about—what parts of the day are adding value to a child's educational experience and what parts are not. In other words, we examine the areas where we can improve our use of time. Like with the stickers—that was one of the ideas that came up as we talked about ways to move the younger children from one activity to another. We take time very seriously because we can never get back time that has been wasted. It is the most precious of precious resources."

At this point, I have a hundred questions for Ms. Young. However, she is ready to dismiss the students for afternoon recess.

Orlo the Wise Old Owl

... on Value-Added Processes

The Lean Enterprise is focused on adding value to the customer. Any activities that do not add value to the customer are considered waste. The sequence of activities that add value to the customer comprise what is called the Value Stream—the flow of the important parts of the process that create the products and services for the customer.

Lean Enterprises put a lot of effort into defining, studying, and improving their Value Streams. It helps to know what needs to be eliminated or improved by separating all your processes or activities into three categories:

Value-added (VA) Activities/Processes: Any activity or process the customer will be willing to pay for. For example, a production worker putting the steering wheel on a car properly would be a value-added process. VA work needs to be optimized and improved upon.

Non-value-added (NVA) Activities/Processes: Any activity or process the customer would not want to pay for if they knew you were doing it. For example, a car manufacturer paying to warehouse 12 months' worth of steering wheels would be non-value-added. NVA work needs to be eliminated.

Business-value-added (BVA) Activities/Processes: Any activity or process the customer would not want to pay for, but which cannot be eliminated at this point. For

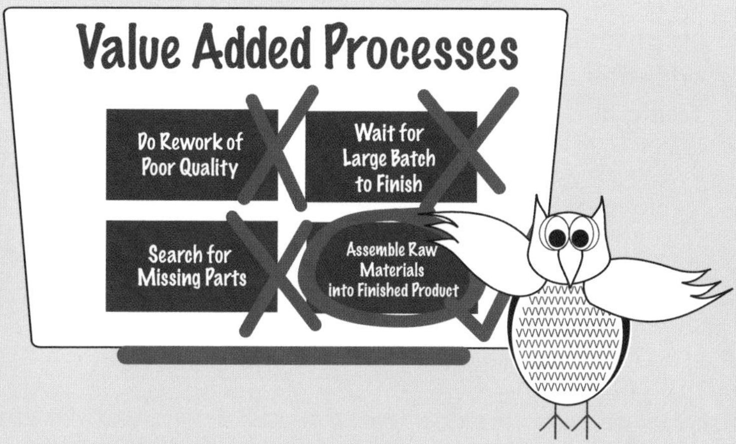

example, legislative and Homeland Security processes may be considered business-value-added. These processes need to be rationalized and then minimized and automated where possible.

In Ms. Young's classroom, instructional time is value-added. Delays caused as students mill about putting away work and getting supplies for another task is mostly non-value-added. In fact, the time it takes to switch from one task to another is a particular area of concern for all kinds of processes because **set-up time**—time used to prepare a process to take on a new kind of work—is non-value-add. Ms. Young's use of the stickers helped her minimize the set-up time for the second activity. Being able to divide the class into subgroups and assign different tasks to different groups helps the class to "parallel process"—which minimizes non-value-add time and gives them more value-add time for their activities.

Having the children go to the bathroom to wash their hands isn't strictly value-added from an instructional viewpoint. But it is necessary for other purposes and therefore qualifies as business-value-add—and as you saw in a previous chapter, Ms. Young had a procedure to minimize that time as well.

Three Lessons on Value

- *Value is defined by the customer and is defined as what they are willing to pay for*
- *Lean organizations work to understand their Value Stream (the main flow of value needed to produce the outcome that customers want)*
- *You must eliminate or at least minimize set-up times and all other activities that do not add value*

2:30 P.M.

A "Go See" Principal

Sitting in a chair designed for a six-year-old gets uncomfortable, so when the class goes out for recess, I decide to stretch my legs. As I reach the classroom door, I almost bump into Mrs. Wright, the principal. I have had some contact with her over the years that my older daughter has attended the school, but I don't know her well.

"Ah," she whispers as she enters the classroom, "I can see by your card that you're a visiting parent. We've met before, haven't we?"

I introduce myself and mention having both an older daughter and a new first grader at her school.

"I'm happy to have you here," she says. "I think it's great when parents take advantage of our offer to spend a day with their child."

"Do many people take you up on the invitation?" I ask.

"Not as many as I'd like," Mrs. Wright sighs. "They get so much out of being here, but not many parents take the time."

"Well, I know that I've been behaving myself," I say with a smile, "but I'd think that having parents wandering through the school would be disruptive."

"Not at all," Mrs. Wright replies. "Our workplace is just like any other. You can't really understand what's happening until you observe the process first-hand. I like parents to get that first-hand look.

"In fact," she adds, "that is why I'm here to observe Ms. Young's class. I get a much better feel for how our teachers and students are doing if I observe the classrooms in action."

"How often do you do this kind of thing?" I ask.

Mrs. Wright answers, "I try to walk around the school, informally observing classrooms and hallway procedures, at least once or twice every day, especially during arrival and dismissal time. I also arrange longer, more formal observations of each teacher according to the school board requirements or if a teacher asks for assistance. School boards set standards for evaluation according to a teacher's previous record and their years of experience."

Knowing that leaders in organizations rarely get into the details, I was surprised by her answer. "Do you really have time for that?" I ask. "With 1,000 students in this school divided into five grades, you have about 40 classrooms, right? I'd think you'd have plenty of other work to do to keep everything coordinated and running smoothly without taking time out to visit classrooms."

Mrs. Wright gives me a smile of understanding, the same smile I suspect she uses with great success on her young students. "Quite the contrary, Robert," she says kindly. "Not only is going into classrooms and walking around the school my favorite activity each day—it's also the most important work that I do."

Mrs. Wright's words conjure up multiple images in my mind. One is of an executive leader who sits in his or her office sending emails to subordinates and managers. Those are leaders who think they know the best way to do something when they have never actually done it themselves or even witnessed the work being done. But I don't want to lose Mrs. Wright's attention so I stop daydreaming and ask her why visiting classrooms is her most important work.

Mrs. Wright raises a hand and counts on her fingers: "First, it gives me a much better understanding of what our teachers experience every day. I learn how our students react to the teaching materials and how different instructional strategies and methods are being used.

"Second," she continues, "knowing what's happening in the classrooms, the gym, and the cafeteria makes it easier for me to discuss our school needs with my staff when we talk about what we need to do to improve. They are far more open to my ideas, and I can better appreciate their struggles and successes when I'm familiar with their reality.

"Third," she adds, "when I speak with parents about their children's day, I can speak with more authority about what is and isn't happening in the school, and I'm better prepared to handle their concerns and suggestions. In fact, I'm often able to prevent an issue or situation from escalating just because I'm there."

I nod my understanding and say, "Come to think of it, I guess that explains why my wife and I get good answers whenever we call to talk to you about our older daughter."

"I know it sounds simple—almost too simple," says Mrs. Wright. "But there's a lot of value in actually going to see how things get done. That's why I encourage parents to visit us, too."

"Do you find that their concerns go away once they visit the school?" I ask.

"Sometimes yes, sometimes no," she answers. "Observing isn't a solution to serious concerns. It's a means of learning more about the reality of a situation or problem. I've found that parents who have observed their child's classroom offer comments that are much more insightful, much better grounded in the reality of what we do every day. They're also much more likely to get involved in helping to identify solutions."

"I totally agree, Mrs. Wright," I reply. "If you want to understand the work, you need to go to where the work is being done."

Orlo the Wise Old Owl

... on "Go See" Management

Leaders inside a Lean Enterprise practice "Go See" management. Before you comment on the state of an operation, you must "Go See" for yourself. Do not rely on what others tell you about the current condition of a process. All people see through a different set of eyes, or have different priorities, and therefore you must create your own opinion by seeing for yourself.

True leaders do not restrict themselves to sitting in their offices all day, every day. Leaders spend their time in the operation, where the work is being done. We call this place the **Gemba**. In the language of Lean, you must "go to the Gemba" often and engage with the people doing the work. This is called **Genchi Gembutsu** (pronounced gen-she gem-boot-sue, with a hard "g" sound at the beginning of both words, as in "guy").

As a leader, you will be extremely surprised that what you *think* is happening and what is *actually* happening can be very different. Only the people directly doing the work truly know what is going on in the operation.

As you spend time in the operation, you will gain respect for and from team members. If you are respected as a leader, you will be seen as more approachable, your staff will be more willing to engage in open dialogue, and they will be more motivated to help drive improvement efforts.

Three Lessons on "Go See" Management

- A leader should spend a significant portion of their time "in the Gemba" (where the work is being done)
- Leaders must observe processes themselves and draw conclusions from their observations
- Leaders talk to the people actually doing the work, because they are the people who truly know what is going on

3:00 P.M.

Where Are the Staples?

I decide to follow Mrs. Wright's suggestion and continue to "learn by seeing." After she gives me permission to wander around the school, I walk out into the hall, leaving behind the first graders as they engage in a learning game. The hallway walls are what you'd expect, decorated with artwork from last year's budding artists and some school slogans.

My previous visits were mostly limited to my elder daughter's classrooms and meetings for parents in the auditorium, so I take this opportunity to familiarize myself with the building's layout. I successfully locate the gymnasium/auditorium and library, and I am on my way back to Abbey's classroom when I pass the office and see a board on the wall behind the main counter. The board displays 3x5 pink cards with writing on them. By concentrating hard and squinting, I read one of the cards.

REORDER:

Standard Staples
StanBosh#: GBS191/4CP
500 staples / box

I just have to ask about this board. "Excuse me," I say to the woman sitting behind the desk, "what are these pink cards on this board behind the counter?"

"Good afternoon, sir," is the reply. "Your card tells me that you're a visiting parent. You're Emilee and Abbey's father, right?"

"Why, yes," I say. "How did you know?"

She says, "All staff are notified when parents are in the building. It's partly a security measure and partly just to make sure we give you the VIP treatment. I recognize you from last year and saw your name on the list of parents here today." She smiles and holds out her hand. "I'm LaDawn. Now what's this about a pink card?"

I point to the board with the pink cards attached.

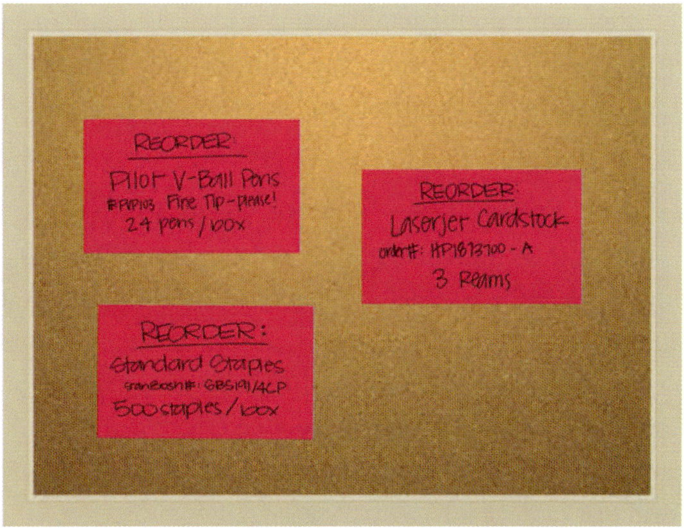

"Ah, yes, that's a management system for our stockroom," LaDawn says. "Let me show you how it works." She walks into the room next door. I've never seen a stockroom so well-organized. LaDawn scans a section that is clearly labeled "staples/staplers."

"See here," she points to a small box on one shelf. "That's where we keep our staples. We put this card on top of the last box. When someone takes the second-to-last box and sees the pink card, they know to stick it onto the "Order" board. Every Thursday, I take the cards off the board and submit an order to our supplier."

"That sounds like a simple system," I say, instantly recognizing what we call a pull-replenishment system in Lean. In this case, they're using 3x5 index cards to act as a trigger system to order more material. With such a trigger, a business doesn't have to order a lot of stuff "just in case"—rather, the material is re-ordered (replenished) when there is a need (the "pull") from the user or customer.

Staying nonchalant despite this discovery, I casually ask, "How did you come up with that plan?"

LaDawn explains that, a few years ago, Mrs. Wright was concerned with increased spending on supplies. "It was a nightmare," she says. "This stock room was messy and overstocked on some items and out-of-stock on others. At one point, we had so many markers in stock that a dozen boxes went dry before we used them. Waste was the last straw for Mrs. Wright. Added to this was the unbelievable growth we have been experiencing. Suddenly, our stockroom was simply too small."

"How did you solve the problem?" I ask.

"I led a team of support staff and teachers who were assigned to study the situation and make suggestions," says LaDawn. "Mrs. Wright said we needed to come up with a solution, as we were the people who used the system."

Under the old system, she goes on to explain, the school ordered supplies for a whole term, which is four months' worth. When all the supplies came in, there wasn't enough storage space, so the storage room became crowded and messy—making it hard for staff to find what they needed. As the term progressed, they'd start running out of certain items, even though the stockroom was jam-packed. In fact, adds LaDawn, they were all incredulous that there were so many supplies in the room but they still seemed to run out of what was needed most.

"Our big 'aha' came when the team realized that we needed a system that would make it easier to tell exactly what we had in stock and what we were running out of," says LaDawn. "At first, we thought we might need to buy some software to manage the stock. But Mrs. Wright would hear nothing of it. That's when we decided to limit supplies kept on hand and to organize and label everything."

"And that's where the 3x5 cards come in?" I ask.

LaDawn points out all the pink cards, one for each item in the room. "Yep. That's how we make sure we don't run out," she replies. "Since we don't have a lot of room for supplies in the building, we were forced to reduce the amount of stock we carried of each item. This meant we had to develop a system that would let us re-order anything and everything that was running low so we could restock before the inventory disappeared completely."

"I'm impressed," I say. "But weren't people worried about running out?"

LaDawn says laughingly, "That's what all the staff said! People were afraid of running out at the beginning, so we kept a 'safety net' as we call it—that's how much back-up we keep around for each item.

"Anyway," she continues with her explanation, "the first year we tried this, we had much higher levels of safety net. There'd be a half-dozen staplers in here, a dozen boxes of staples, a chest-high stack of boxes of paper, and on and on for each item."

"Did that help make sure you didn't run out?" I ask.

"No," she replies, "and we also discovered that the safety net hid the problems with our new system. For example, we had a hard time telling just how fast we were using up various supplies."

"What did you do?"

"We realized that we received supplies from our supplier sporadically, in big batches, and without any pattern of delivery," says LaDawn. "So we went to our supplier and asked them to start making deliveries once per week. That helped us keep lower stock levels and better monitor how much we used."

"And what happened?" I ask.

"Over time, two things happened," she answers. "First, we got better and better at predicting how much of what items we really needed at which times of the year. We started ordering smaller amounts of supplies more often. Staff began trusting the system, knowing that we could get items in quickly if necessary. So each year we've been able to trim back on the safety net in the stockroom."

"It sounds like it's worked well for you," I say, impressed by how simple she makes the system sound.

"Our team was very proud of the results," says LaDawn. "That first year, we cut supply costs by 10 percent and we expect to achieve a savings of 35 percent this year. The staff and teachers rave about how much faster they can find what they want. This year we're going to look at reducing inventory by 50 percent and we want to reduce the variety of items we order. We have a lot of different kinds of pens and paper, for example. We think we can get the teachers and support staff to pick a few standard items."

"Have you thought about having your supplier deliver every day, or at least several times a week?" I ask. "That way you could get rid of most of the material in this room and use it for some other purpose!"

"That's a great idea," says LaDawn. "I'll bring up that idea to the staff. We've been trying to arrange to have a separate space where student teams can meet during the day!"

"You've done a fantastic job already," I reply. "I'm getting more and more confident that my tax dollars are being used wisely at this school!" At that point, I realize I'd better get back to Abbey's class.

Orlo the Wise Old Owl

... on Pull-Replenishment

As mentioned before, the Lean Enterprise understands that overproduction is the king of waste. Whether in manufacturing, distribution, or an office, overproduction is when we make or buy more than we need at that time. Overproduction is also when we make or buy items before we actually need them. Overproduction creates the waste of excess inventories, which are very expensive to store, move, count, correct... and the list goes on. Overproduction is nothing but a drain on resources.

The Lean method to eliminate overproduction and reduce inventories is to implement a concept known as **supply chain velocity.**

Velocity is created by moving smaller quantities of material more frequently with standard, leveled (meaning they are the same quantity over the available time), and consistent timing. Velocity will reduce the amount of inventory you need to keep on hand. As you reduce inventory levels, you will begin to expose problems that have been hidden by the inventory. And as we have learned, exposing problems is good news.

The mechanisms for achieving supply chain velocity are **improving flow** and moving to a **pull-replenishment** system. *Pull* simply means that we only replenish material and information when it has been consumed, and only in the quantity that has been consumed.

In other words, in a pull system, consumption is what triggers replenishment. Contrast that to typical "push" systems used in most organizations where the amount of supplies or materials ordered (or produced) is based on batch thinking, forecasting, and guessing. The result is inventory that is not required (but that you have to pay for!). The worst part in a push system is that you will have a lot of inventory, but not the items you need on a given day or in the quantity you need.

Implementing pull systems does not need to be overly complicated. As you saw, Williams Elementary makes their supply-replacement visible using a simple 3x5 card system. In Lean manufacturing such a "pull card" is known as a **Kanban** (pronounced kahn-bon). The Kanban is attached to material and tells a team member when material should be produced or replenished. Pull systems do not need to be based on complex technology. Keep it simple and keep it visual.

Three Lessons on "Pull"

- Replenishment of inventory should be triggered by actual consumption, not by forecasts and guessing
- Pull-Replenishment systems can be simple and inexpensive
- Pull-Replenishment systems help you level the amount of activity across an entire process, reduce inventory (and hence reduce costs), and expose problems

How Did We Do?

3:30 P.M.

It is nearing the end of the school day and Ms. Young is reviewing the three rules that govern school and classroom behavior.

"Who can remember the three rules I talked about this morning?" she asks. Several students raise their hands. She calls on a curly-haired boy sitting near the back.

"We have to follow the school rules," he says.

"Yes, Sammy. You're right. For example, one of the important rules in this school is to behave in the lunchroom," Ms. Young says. "Now that you have been to the lunchroom, do you know why that rule is important?"

A girl in a print dress raises her hand. When Ms. Young acknowledges her she says with a giggle, "So the boys don't chase us around."

"It's not just the boys we don't want running around, Cecilia," Ms. Young replies. She then calls on a very serious boy in the fourth row. "George, why do you think running around in the cafeteria would be against the rules?"

George shrugs his shoulders and says, "Maybe we could trip and fall and spill a bunch of food all over the place."

"That's right, George," says Ms. Young. "We don't want anyone to go home with spaghetti sauce on their shirt." The class giggles. "OK, everyone, why else should we behave in the lunchroom?"

Ms. Young continues the discussion for several minutes, getting the children to talk about ideas like getting through lunch quickly so there is more time for both their studies and recess. She then goes back to her first question. "Those are all great ideas, children. Now can anyone remember the other rules we talked about this morning?"

This time Abbey speaks up, making her dad proud. "We have to be nice to each other," she states with confidence.

"Perfect, Abbey, you are right. We want people in this school to be nice to each other," repeats Ms. Young. "We have to treat each other with respect. Does anyone know what respect means?"

The class shows surprising maturity and the discussion continues for some time. They talk about being nice to each other and helping to make their classroom and their school a safe and happy place. When Ms. Young asks for the third rule, the class discusses the importance of listening, learning, and working hard in class.

Ms. Young looks at the clock and says, "Class, it is time to listen to the announcements. Our principal, Mrs. Wright, is going to talk to us now."

There is a crackling noise and Mrs. Wright's voice comes over the speaker. "Good afternoon. As you know, every day for the first month of school, I announce the winner of our Williams' Wizards Award. The winner today is Ms. Young's first grade class, room 101. You have done an excellent job of following the school rules on the first day of school! Congratulations to the children and to Ms. Young."

Ms. Young, the children, and I are shocked; it takes a few moments for this news to sink in. The next minute we are smiling, cheering, and congratulating each other on our successful day. I will always remember the look of joy and amazement on Abbey's face. The students feel so proud. I can see their self-confidence building right in front of my eyes. In that moment, every one of these children knows what it feels like to be a good student.

Orlo the Wise Old Owl

... on Communication and Feedback

The Lean Enterprise understands the value of effective communication and providing feedback to all team members in the organization. Communication is not different from any other process in the business. Like all processes, there are inputs, procedures, timing, and outputs. Therefore, when it comes to communication, you need to know:

1. **What do we need to communicate?** (inputs) *Here, the focus was on the three core values of the school.*

2. **How are we going to communicate?** (procedures) *Each teacher was to talk about the values with their class to make sure every student understood.*

3. **When and with what frequency will we communicate?** (timing) *Williams Elementary made a discussion about values part of every day for the first full month of school, then less frequently after that.*

4. **What is the expected action or result from this communication?** (outputs) *The students were expected to understand the values, raise questions when they didn't understand, and shape their behavior to conform to the values.*

People require and rightfully deserve feedback. The Lean Enterprise holds respect for people in the highest of priorities. Good or bad, it is the duty of the organization to have mechanisms to deliver feedback to all employees. People want to know the vision, strategies, and goals of the organization. People want to know if/when they are doing well and where they need to improve. It is not sufficient for only top management to have a high level of understanding of the status of the business. All team members need to know what is going on and how their personal contribution fits into the greater good of the business.

Three Lessons on Communication

- To respect people, you need to have open, honest, and frequent communication
- Communication is a process with inputs, outputs, procedures, and timing
- All people need to know where they stand and how they impact the business

Going Home Prepared

Ms. Young's class is abuzz with the news that they have won the Williams' Wizards Award for the day.

"I'm very proud of you," Ms. Young says. "What a great way to start the new school year! Now, we have two more things to do before the last bell." She begins handing out sheets of paper.

"This is your weekly To Do list," says Ms. Young. "I will be giving you one of these orange sheets each week. Put your sheet in your folder along with the drawing you made today. Remember to give your folder to your parents and to share your work with them. This information helps your parents help you, so that you will come to school each day well prepared to learn.

"For example," she continues, "some days I'll be asking you to do some work at home before you come back to school the next day. When I do, I'll write out exactly what I want you to do on the orange sheet. Other days, you may need to bring in special supplies from home, and that will be listed. Or if we're going to take special field trips, like the one to the zoo next week, those will be on the orange sheet, too. I'll also write down when we're going to have quizzes or tests. Does anybody have any questions?"

"Do we have to bring the orange sheet back?" asks one girl.

"No, Rita, these orange sheets are just for you and your parents," answers Ms. Young. "OK, class? Look at your orange sheet and we will read it together." She guides the children through the reading, then asks, "Are there any questions? If your parents have questions, ask them to email or phone me."

Ms. Young begins walking around the room; she is talking about the items on the orange sheet and answering the children's questions. One homework assignment is listed. Students are asked to bring in empty aluminum cans for an art project on Friday.

"The last thing we will do each day is go over the activity board to review what we did today and to see our plan for tomorrow," states Ms. Young. Together, the class goes through today's events, recalling and discussing the high and lows of the day. They talk about how they will repeat the things that worked well and how they will improve upon the things that did not work so well. Then she reads through the schedule for the next day, asking and reminding the children about the symbols.

Just as she finishes, the bell rings to signal the end of the school day. Kids scramble for the door. Ms. Young tells them to slow down, "Children, remember, we don't want anyone to get hurt. Safety first! See you all tomorrow."

While Abbey is collecting her things from her cubbyhole, I watch Ms. Young open a book on her desk.

Curious, I ask what she is doing and she tells me that she is making some debriefing notes for the day.

"Most teachers keep a daybook," she explains. "There are different ways of doing this and, with experience, teachers adapt their daybook to suit their needs and the needs of their pupils."

She goes on to explain that some teachers start with a template that matches the student's activity chart or, for higher grades, their subject schedules. Her template matches the weekly schedule on the activity board except she uses words instead of images. Each subject and timeframe contains a space in which she writes a brief sketch of the lesson plan for that subject for that day.

"At the end of the day," she concludes, "I check off what has been completed and circle what has not. I also make notes to myself that will be helpful for the next day."

"Is it worth it?" I ask Ms. Young.

"This daybook has many purposes," she answers. "One is that it serves as a plan for a substitute teacher. Suppose tomorrow I'm ill and can't come to school. The teacher who takes charge of this classroom will have a record of what was done in each subject today and what is planned for tomorrow. For example, under mathematics, the skill and the skill level will be entered along with page numbers from student arithmetic workbooks and teacher manuals or reference materials, which will be stacked on the desk."

"Does managing a classroom take a lot of time? It seems like a lot of record keeping that takes a lot of work and discipline," I say as I try to get my head around the speed at which Ms. Young is able to fill in her daybook.

"Not really," she replies, "the daybook is part of my routine and because it is a working document, it is flexible and helpful. I am free to write as much or as little as I need. This is not a report or a 'pretty' document for show, although it is a document that provides a permanent record of what my plan was and what actually happened in a day. I see it as a running record of our accomplishments, successes, and challenges. It also helps me set a direction for future planning."

Ms. Young goes on to say that her system helps her focus on priorities each day. "The end-of-day checklist and reminders are probably the most important parts of my system. It's nothing too complicated—I don't have time for that. Today, for instance, I'll jot down that talking with the students about the school rules and classroom organization went well. I'll also note that Table 6 may need more guidance or help when I ask them to make a decision within their group. I'll make a note to observe Brian's and Lisa's behavior and perhaps next time I will provide more coaching so they can do better at working together."

She starts packing up her notebook. "I also use this system to jot down notes about my students, such as their interests or hobbies outside of school, or things I pick up on from their drawings," she adds. "Individual details about students are helpful when I'm choosing read-aloud material for the class or books for their silent reading."

At this point in the conversation, Abbey is tugging on my sleeve.

Orlo the Wise Old Owl

... on Plan-Do-Check-Act

The hardest part of creating a Lean Enterprise is sustaining change after it is implemented. Sustaining Lean improvements is difficult because:

- Organizations do not stay on task; they tend to lose focus
- Organizations don't fight waste every minute of the day

Like everything else in life, strategy and focus will naturally move off course unless they are constantly attended to. Waste wants to grow. It is as if strategy and waste are living organisms and their job is to grow off course each day. Therefore, you need to exert pressure every minute to hold waste back and to keep strategy deployment on track. The best way to accomplish this is to use the Scientific Model, also known as the **Plan-Do-Check-Act cycle** (PDCA).

While it is called a scientific model, it is simple to understand and to implement. You start by making sure you have a plan for every process in the business. During the day, you do your plan. Then you check the results to compare your plan versus what actually happened that day. The gap between plan and actual is considered a problem. You adjust your processes accordingly and start the PDCA process all over again. The power of PDCA is when it becomes part of the business culture. Effective PDCA may be the deciding factor between a successful or unsuccessful Lean Journey.

Three Lessons on Maintaining Gains

- Strategy and focus will deteriorate if you do not pay regular attention to them
- We must fight every day to keep strategy on course and waste from growing
- A simple method like the Plan-Do-Check-Act problem-solving cycle will create the foundation for Lean sustainment

Soccer Practice

4:00 P.M.

C'mon, Dad, are you ready to go?" Abbey is once again standing by, waiting for me to catch up. "I'm going to be late for soccer practice," she says plaintively.

"Soccer practice, did I know about that?" I ask.

"Well, we talked about it last night. Mom made sure I packed my soccer shoes this morning," Abbey answers. "See, they're right here in my backpack."

"We'd better hurry. Get a move on!" I try to make it sound like she is the one causing the delay, but I don't think she buys into my act.

By the time we make it out to the soccer fields behind the school, most of the other children and parents are already there. Abbey drops her backpack on the ground beside me. I help her with her shoes, and then she hurries off to join the other first and second graders. They are clustered around a young woman with a whistle, obviously the coach, who quickly gets the younger students organized into drills to practice the basic skills. I notice that the teams of older students are doing the same.

About 20 minutes later, the coach divides the first and second graders into two groups and has them try playing a game against each other. I watch Abbey's team, trying not to laugh at them as they all scramble after the ball at the same time—except for a few who are standing stock still or picking grass, apparently waiting for the ball to come to them. When kids at this age play soccer, there is little hope of anyone scoring—except by accident.

It is a chaotic scene. At this point, I look over at the teams of third and fourth graders. The older kids obviously have learned how to play positions. They seem to know that having different positions played properly increases the odds of scoring a goal—but what's interesting is how these kids stand rigidly in position, seemingly not doing anything unless the ball comes *to* them! It reminds me of a tabletop "dome hockey" game I had when I was a kid living up north in Timmins, Ontario. The players on the hockey board could only go so far up and down the board in their individual track, so you would only use a player when it could reach the puck.

What's worse, I wonder to myself—having an entire team chase the ball all over the field or having a team of players who stand still until the ball comes directly to their spot?

I glance over to the fifth graders playing on another field. They are clearly moving the ball up and down the soccer field with more advanced skill and efficiency.

What are they doing differently? I ask myself.

As I watch more closely, I see that, for starters, they are not chasing the ball in clusters. They are playing specific positions—in principle, what the third and fourth graders are doing—but each player seems to know if and when it is his or her responsibility to go for the ball. I also realize what the oldest kids are doing to move the ball around so well: While some kids are obviously assigned to chase the ball, others are playing specific positions. But any of the kids can leave their position when it makes sense to the flow of the play. In other words, there is a discipline to stay in a position, but the kids are flexible—if circumstances change, they leave their position to support a fellow team member.

I can't help but draw a parallel to what happens so often inside organizations. On one hand, companies are simply chasing the ball in a cluster, fighting the latest fire. The whole organization is just trying to get through the day. In this situation, processes are unstable, strategic objectives have no way of being met, and people cannot work on improving the business—they are too busy using brute force to meet customer needs.

On the other hand, many organizations have each employee playing inside the limited boundaries of their individual position, worrying only about their functional silo and not understanding how their position interacts with and impacts the rest of the business. When employees have no concept of the larger game plan, their decisions may be good for their specific job, role, or department, but run counter to something that is better for the organization as a whole. Creating an environment where employees understand the larger game will help the company make better decisions overall.

In reality, real teamwork and positive results happen when we stabilize processes, stop fighting fires, and think of the business as a system or a structure of interconnected parts. Each part relies on the others for the ultimate success of the organization. Therefore, people need to know their personal roles in the organization, but they also need to be able to offer suggestions and feedback to others in the organization. People need to be able to move around in the organization when it makes sense.

With this thought in mind, I remember times in my life when I got defensive if somebody offered a suggestion about how I might manage my area better. My first thought and response was: *you have enough problems in your own department, who are you to tell me what I should do?* But, thinking back now, those people in other departments felt the effects of my work. In reality, they were the best ones to tell me what I needed to improve.

My daydreaming about the destructive elements of departmental silos and human defensiveness is abruptly interrupted as Abbey begins tugging on my sleeve once again.

"Soccer practice is over, Daddy," she alerts me.

"Great, honey," I say. As we walk away from the soccer field I ask, "So, Abbey, did you have a good first day of first grade?"

"I sure did, Dad," Abbey replies.

I add with sincerity, "So did I, honey, so did I. Now let's go home."

Orlo the Wise Old Owl

... on Teamwork and Collaboration

The Lean Enterprise is built on the principles of teamwork and true collaboration. This means that all people in the organization need to understand the vision and work together toward common goals. Teamwork and improvement will happen if people know and follow the standards for their work—and know when/how to change those standards for the better!—and if they are allowed to make suggestions for improvement in all areas of the business.

Notice from the story how the soccer teams progressed. The youngest students simply chased the ball as a group with no strategy or awareness of position. The next level of soccer players recognized that positions are important, however they believed that having a position meant they could not move around the playing field, even when it made sense to do so. The oldest children, whose teams are most effective, know to not chase the ball, to play a position, and also to move around the field when it will benefit the entire team.

Once you progress to a mature stage of effective teamwork, problems will be consistently identified and eliminated through collaboration.

Once you realize that the Lean culture is about identifying and solving problems, you will stop becoming defensive when people point out weaknesses in your operation. You need to collaborate and respect the fact that others may see problems and opportunities that you don't see because you are too close to the details. Remember that you cannot solve all problems by yourself. The best way to improve the business is to create teams of individuals from all levels in the organization. They need to be people who sincerely want to work together to get the job done.

Three Lessons on Teamwork

- *Teamwork and collaboration requires people from all levels of the organization to be working toward common goals*
- *Teamwork is created when people know the standards for their own work and are encouraged to move around in the business to offer suggestions to others*
- *For true teamwork to take place, people must not be defensive about constructive criticism as the goal of the Lean culture is to identify and fix problems*

Reflections

I drive Abbey home. She puts her backpack by the door and goes out to play while Corinne and I prepare dinner. During the meal, Abbey tells stories about her first day of first grade to her mother. After dinner, she gets out her folder and shows her mother the drawing she made and the orange sheet for parents.

Corinne asks me if I enjoyed the day with Abbey. I tell her in all honesty that it was an amazing day.

"Yes," she says. "I knew you would enjoy it. You needed a day away from work and from thinking about Lean all the time!" I smile at her, and think—*if she only knew*.

Soon Corinne and I are snuggled up with Abbey reading a bedtime story as we do every night. I can't help but reflect on the day.

Like everything around us, our schools have evolved in their thinking and approaches to educating our children. However, there are certain guiding principles that seem to be timeless, as well as critical, to a successful learning experience. Students learn better when they feel comfortable and secure, when they are self-confident, and when they believe in their ability to learn. Abbey and other children wouldn't express it in this way, but her full-time job in first grade is to learn. This is the same in our business organizations. How can we expect to grow and to prosper if we are not learning each and every day?

Remembering Abbey's school, I think about the visual cues, standard routines, classroom organization, and the problem-solving exercises. What are schools attempting to accomplish? I arrive at the conclusion that these tactics are simply tools to create a fertile learning environment, one where Abbey and her classmates can learn to the best of each of their abilities. The teachers, the principal, the entire school's infrastructure is designed to help students learn each and every day.

It's apparent that not all children or adults learn at the same pace or in the same way. However, we learn better when we are fully engaged in the process and when we are given opportunities to problem solve on our own and within a team.

Like a school, a Lean Enterprise is a culture where the opportunity to learn, to take risks, to problem solve, and to work as a team is embedded in the daily routines and processes. No matter our age, we thrive on being part of a bigger solution and knowing that our opinions and ideas matter.

At the end of the day, when we filter out the noise, learning is the most important component of the human experience.

Conclusion & Author's Comments

I sincerely hope you enjoyed the story.

This story is the result of several visits to Abbey's class. While I have used creative license in places to support Lean concepts, the descriptions closely match the activities in an actual, progressive first grade classroom. Some examples of the inspirational work is shown in the photos on these pages.

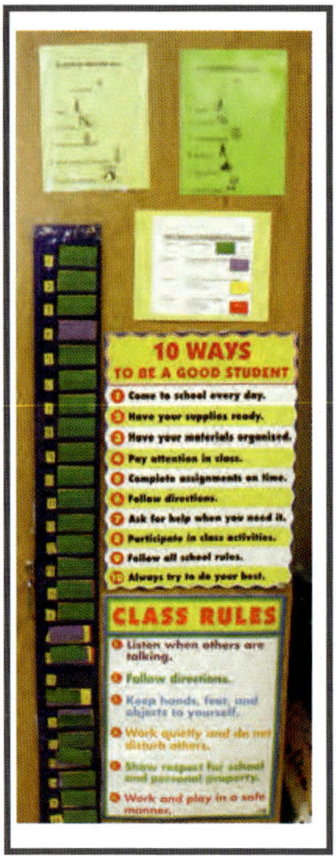

I know for certain that readers will think the "Henry Ford" song is fiction, but believe me, I literally fell off my chair.

I enjoyed every minute of this book project. It allowed me to spend time with Abbey and Emilee, to discuss the concept of Lean in first grade with colleagues and family, and to organize and confirm my own thoughts and ideas about Lean.

In writing this book, it was very important to me that this story add value to the reader. If I can accomplish one thing with this book, it is to illustrate that Lean is about thinking and learning, and not simply im-

More of the work that inspired this story.

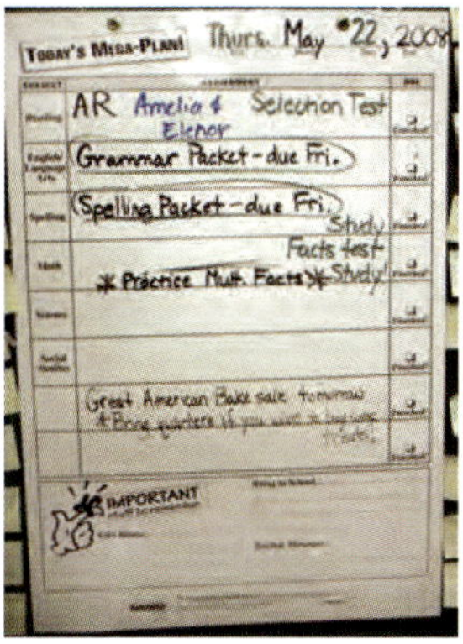

plementing a set of tools. If you are now motivated to go organize an area of your work, and you also understand why you would do this, then I have met my objective. The why is more critical then the how. As I mentioned in the introduction, without knowing why, the how will never be sustained.

As I also mentioned in my introduction, becoming a student of Lean can and will have a permanent effect on you. With that, I end this book with a story that happened to me recently.

A few Saturdays ago, I woke up knowing the plan was for me to spend the day with Emilee and Abbey. I had just come off a stretch of significant travel, so quality time with my girls was due. I was up for anything they wanted to do. The three of us sat down at the breakfast table to plan our day.

"What should we do today?" I asked both girls.

They looked at each other and Emilee said, "Let's brainstorm!"

At that point, Abbey responded, "Great idea, I'll get the whiteboard!"

I fell off my chair! (This happens a lot.)

Abbey came back with her small portable whiteboard and both girls started writing ideas for our day on the board. At one point, Emilee suggested we go to the zoo.

Abbey responded with, "I don't want to go to the zoo!"

And within two seconds, Emilee replied, "Abbey, in brainstorming, no idea is a bad idea!"

Ah, thank goodness for the gift of learning, and the gift of family.

Good luck on your Lean Journey and may you learn each and every day.

Robert Orloe Martichenko
30 June 2008

About the Author

Robert Martichenko is the Founder and CEO of LeanCor Supply Chain Group.

He is a supply chain leader and educator who's focused his entire career on third party logistics. Beginning in transportation and warehousing, Robert continued his career learning and implementing lean and operational excellence with a focus on end to end supply chain management.

This experience allowed him to found LeanCor for the sole purpose of supporting customers to advance their supply chains. Additionally, Robert has written several books and publications on lean supply chain management, and serves as a senior instructor for the Georgia Tech Supply Chain and Logistics Institute and the Lean Enterprise Institute.

Please contact Robert at **RMartichenko@leancor.com** and please visit **www.leancor.com**.

About the Illustrator

Liz Maute is an artist of all sorts from Norman, Oklahoma.

She graduated from the University of Oklahoma with a bachelor's degree in journalism and mass communications with an emphasis on advertising. She is a graphic designer for print and web and keeps a portfolio online at www.lizmaute.com.

Liz also has a blog about design at lizzicious.wordpress.com.

Armed with nothing but a craft knife in her tiny apartment kitchen/dining room, Liz created the images for this story by cutting thousands of tiny pieces of paper and gluing them all together before scanning the figures into Photoshop for final editing. The video of how the illustrations were made is available online at www.youtube.com/lizmaute.

Liz has also made over 300 one-of-a-kind frames and other various home décor items. More information is available online at www.hautemaute.com.